The
BEST YEAR
OF YOUR LIFE

The
BEST YEAR
OF YOUR LIFE

Dream It, Plan It, Live It

Debbie Ford

HarperOne
An Imprint of HarperCollins Publishers

HarperOne

THE BEST YEAR OF YOUR LIFE: *Dream It, Plan It, Live It*. Copyright © 2005 by Debbie Ford. All rights reserved. Printed in the United States of America. No part of this book may be used or reproduced in any manner whatsoever without written permission except in the case of brief quotations embodied in critical articles and reviews. For information, address HarperCollins Publishers, 195 Broadway, New York, NY 10007.

HarperCollins books may be purchased for educational, business, or sales promotional use. For information,please e-mail the Special Markets Department at SPsales@harpercollins.com.

HarperCollins Web site: http://www.harpercollins.com

HarperCollins®, 🍰®, and HarperOne™ are trademarks of HarperCollins Publishers.

FIRST HARPERCOLLINS PAPERBACK EDITION PUBLISHED IN 2006

Designed by Kris Tobiassen

Library of Congress Cataloging-in-Publication Data

Ford, Debbie.
   The best year of your life : dream it, plan it, live it / Debbie Ford.—1st ed.
   ISBN: 978-0-06-083294-0
   1. Self-actualization (Psychology)   I. Title.
   BF637.S4F64 2004
   158.1—dc22

                                                              2004054079

      17 18 19 RRD(H) 20 19 18 17 16 15

To my brilliant and good-hearted son,
Beau Bressler,
whose unconditional love makes every year my best year.
I thank God every day for the blessing of you.

CONTENTS

CONTENTS

Live It

Creating the Best Year of Your Life

*E*very year around the world, most of us participate in the same New Year's ritual. This ritual
does not involve celebrating, dancing, drinking, or being
with loved ones. It's not about reflecting on our past or
even being grateful for what we have in our lives. This
New Year's tradition is simply the ritual of making a resolution to change, a promise to ourselves to do something
new or different. Whether we're pledging to improve our
finances, our relationships, our appearance, or our employ-
ment, what we all share is one common desire—to make
this year better than our last.

So what happens? Why does our resolve fade so quickly? Why do most of us fail to achieve our desired goals? Why are they mostly forgotten or abandoned by February? Is it that we no longer want the things we thought were so important on January 1? Have our goals and objectives changed? Have we thrown in the towel and given up? Or do we fail simply because we never put into place the plans, structure, and tools we need to succeed?

But what if this year is different? What if you live each day of the coming year with the rock-solid intent to make it the best year of your life—no matter what happens, no matter what uncontrollable forces intervene, no matter what changes around you take place? What if you discover that having the best year of your life is something that is completely within your own control, something that you can actually shape, create, and achieve? What if today you realize that the choice is really yours?

The possibility of making this your best year ever exists in every moment, because having the best year of your life depends not on some outside accomplishment but on allowing the greatest expression of yourself to be unveiled. Having the best year of your life is about becoming the person you always wanted to be. It's about embracing a vision of yourself at your best and developing the qualities that will take you there.

In the same way an artist reveals the beautiful sculpture that is hidden within a block of marble, each of us must chip away at the outer layers that prevent us from seeing and becoming our true selves. With the passion of a world-class sculptor, we each must make a commitment to chip away at our self-imposed limitations and take the time to discover the ways we have hidden our talents and covered up our deepest desires. To create the best year of our lives, we must challenge our self-defeating behaviors and find new ways of reacting to the everyday events that shape our experience. We must first digest and embrace all the limiting beliefs we've collected throughout the years, and then, ultimately, summon the courage to let go of them all—everything that is covering our true masterpiece. To live our best year, we must take the time to explore the thought process that has shaped our ability to succeed or fail, to rise to our finest self or sink into mediocrity.

Most of us have put some kind of limitations on what we can and cannot have, what we can and cannot do, and who we can and cannot be. We resign ourselves to the fact that each year will be either the same or only slightly better than our last, rather than letting ourselves get excited about a limitless future. We construct boundaries around our ambitions, our goals, and our imaginations. And we forfeit total self-expression in favor of fitting in with the masses. As adults, most of us have shut off the child in us, giving up fun-loving pranks and repressing our tireless imaginations. We've traded in our roller skates and times of skipping in the streets for more serious tasks. Our state of curiosity has been replaced by righteous thinking that restricts what we hear and what we see. Our open and loving nature has been replaced by a guarded and defended heart. And, instead of joyfully going about the task of making the lives we are living great, we daydream about the life we wish we were living.

Maybe you have slipped into the pattern of waiting for the day when your fantasy life will arrive. You might be hoping that the day is coming when you will finally have more success, money, love, or happiness. Like so many, you may be waiting for something to happen tomorrow that will make you feel better about your life today. But I ask you, has that tomorrow shown up yet?

It's time to break through the illusion that the best year of your life exists somewhere out there, in the future, when the reality is that it exists right here and now. Don't get fooled into thinking for one more minute that the best year of your life will just happen . . . if you are lucky. Don't believe that you lack what it takes to make this a great year, no matter what you are doing or what is happening in your life. Don't wait for everything to be done, for your schedule to get cleared, or for your dream man or woman to appear before you take on the task of creating a life you love. Don't let the fantasy of "One day . . ." or "Next year . . ." or "When I have more time . . ." or "When I have more money . . ." trick you into believing that the best year of your life exists somewhere off in the future.

It is your choice, here and now. Just think about it: This life is available to you whether you are alone, sick, fat, poor, busy, depressed, or addicted. It can be yours even if you don't have a proper education, even if you've done some bad things in the past, even if you have flaws in your personality, even if you were abandoned by someone you loved or beaten as a child, even if you feel unsupported by your loved ones, and even if things around you appear to be out of your control. Your best year is not about getting all the things you think you need to be happy. It's not about finishing that project or finding the love of your life or losing those twenty pounds. It's not about getting out of debt or landing that new job. In fact, in the year to come you could lose a loved one or a job. You could get divorced or run into obstacles in your career. But what I hope to show you is that having the best year of your life does not require that every day be a rosy land of paradise or that everything go your way. What it does require is for you to develop those parts of yourself that are yearning to be expressed. The best year of your life is about becoming inspired by yourself, loving who you are and the choices you're making. It's about making peace with your past so that you can create a future that is unlike anything you have ever experienced. It's about living each day grounded in reality, with passion and excitement for life, and inspiring others to do the same.

The best year of your life is possible no matter what is going on around you. It is yours for the taking. This year, you get to choose what actions you will take and what behaviors you will engage in. You get to choose, in response to the issues you are dealing with, whether you will give up your right to have everything you desire, settling for the illusion of ease that comes from blindly repeating the past—or whether you will tread a new path.

Although at first glance this process might seem daunting, it is really much simpler than you might think, because it is one of surrender. It's the process of letting go of your stories, excuses, and self-imposed limitations. Living your best year calls on you to surrender your outdated beliefs about what you are capable of being or doing and to replace them with the belief that your job is to be the greatest expression of yourself, knowing that there is no finer contribution you can make to this world than fulfilling your highest potential.

The Best Year of Your Life is a call to action. It's a step-by-step guide to making this year so special that you can't wait to jump out of bed in the morning and begin your day. The intent of this book is to inspire, nurture, and support you in attaining a level of joy that you may not even know is possible for you and to leave you, at the end of the year, wanting more of what you have already created. *The Best Year of Your Life* is your personal guide to living your greatest life, no matter what is going on around you. Its job is to support you in defining what the best year of your life means to you—what it will look and feel like—and to support you in creating it. Once you are in the presence of your best life, this book will show you how to design a powerful plan to ensure your success and gather the skills you need to fulfill your long-awaited dreams.

We will begin in the "Dream It" section, where we will reawaken to our deepest desires and use them to discover the persons we have always wanted to be. We will learn what it means to live inside an intent to create the best year of our lives and to open up to the possibility of living a year beyond our wildest dreams. We will create a future grounded in reality rather than fantasy and reclaim the power to give ourselves everything we have been chasing, whether it's success, importance, validation, love, or happiness. We will come to the startling and life-changing realization that what we have been chasing in the outer world can be generated within ourselves, giving us immediate access to that which we desire. Then we will allow a vision of ourselves at our highest to unfold and propel us to the life we long to lead.

In the "Plan It" section, we will clean our slates and prepare the fertile ground in which we will plant and nurture our new and inspiring futures. We'll break down our visions for our best year into attainable goals and design a detailed map that, when followed step-by-step, will ensure that we will arrive at our desired destination.

Finally, in the "Live It" section, we gain the courage to create and seize all the days of the coming year and claim them as the best days of our lives. We will learn a special technique for capturing the priceless moments that give our lives meaning and for basking in the joy of what we already have. We'll learn the exciting process of how to live inside our personal integrity, which ensures that we will stay on the straight line of success in the coming year. Our personal integrity will support us in making choices that are consistent with the person we desire to be and will act as our inner compass—our guide, so to speak—making sure that we stay true to ourselves and arrive at the doorstep of our deepest desires. We will come to the understanding that the best year of our lives is built upon a foundation of feeling good about who we are, what we do, and how we do it. This understanding will inspire us to live each day in a way that leaves us feeling proud and confident about who we are.

Right now, you have a choice. You can make this year, this day, this moment a demarcation and declare that this will be the best year of your life, or you can continue down the same old road you've been down so many times before. This book provides a simple, life-changing, and proven process that will allow you to create, starting today, *the best year of your life*. If you follow this process, it will ensure that having your best year yet will be more than a pipe dream; it will be your destiny.

Whether you begin this journey on January 1 or on your birthday or on some Sunday in October, today you have the power to make this the beginning of your finest year yet. I hope it is clear that you possess this power. Having the best year of your life is your right—it is your birthright—and you have the power to make it happen.

If you're tired of mediocrity, if you cannot tolerate one more year of the same, I invite you to commit, to challenge yourself and to join me in creating *the best year of your life.*

The
BEST YEAR
OF YOUR LIFE

Dream It

Cherish your visions and your dreams, as they are the children of your soul—the blueprints of your ultimate accomplishments.

—NAPOLEON HILL

ONE

Creating a
Powerful Intent

*I*magine waking up each morning with an excitement and passion that you haven't felt in years. Imagine going through each day, enjoying every moment, feeling purposeful and fulfilled. This is what you can expect if you live each day, week, and month of this year to its fullest—if you show up at each moment with the commitment to use all of your gifts, talents, and brilliance. This is exactly what you will experience if you bring forth the intent to have the best year of your life.

Like all great accomplishments, this life-changing journey must begin with a single step: *You must create a conscious intent for this to be the best year of your life.* An intent is a commitment to yourself to bring into existence a particular result. It is the driving force, the hidden compass, that directs your daily behaviors. A conscious intent acts as an organizing principle, guiding you to make empowering choices. It ensures that you are indeed the captain of your own ship, and it gives you the power to choose your destination. Intent precedes manifestation. With a powerful, conscious intent, you can chart your journey through life with clarity and focus, and choose the particular reality you want to create.

Intent is to humans what software is to a computer. When installed into your psyche, intent gives you access to new capabilities, which opens up new realities. Suddenly you are able to see your life through new eyes. When you powerfully choose to insert into your consciousness the intent to have the best year of your life— to load it into your hard drive, so to speak—you will see your life as you never have before. You will instantly have access to making changes instead of just talking about them. When you load the intent to have the best year of your life, you are choosing to bring into existence a life filled with love, laughter, success, and fulfillment. Following is an example that beautifully illustrates the power of intent.

Julia is a talented, vivacious woman who worked for my coaching organization for over two years. She liked her job and was good at what she did. She was happy and healthy, and had wonderful friends. By anyone's standards Julia was living a great life. Then, a year and a half ago, I offered to lead my staff through a "Best Year of Your Life" training. In the course of the training, Julia, along with the others, created the intent to have the best year of her life. Looking through the lens of having the coming year be her best year yet, Julia saw that she would have to make some immediate changes. Her first realization, which came as a surprise to both of us, was that she would have to quit her job and create a new career doing exactly what she loves to do: coaching others and playing golf. She also saw that if she was going to live her best year she would have to move to a place that inspired and uplifted her. Just by taking an hour to explore what her finest year would look like, Julia saw that she would have to make some major changes in two key areas of her life. Her new intent had allowed her to see what she couldn't see before. With great enthusiasm Julia explained, "I feel like I've been living in a little box and somebody just took the lid off and said, 'Hey, there is a whole big world out there and there are a thousand other options that you've never even considered.'"

Six months later, almost every aspect of Julia's life was completely unrecognizable. Her intent to have her finest year yet inspired her to move to a quaint little coastal town that she adores and to follow her passion for golf. She is now the founder and president of Championship Inner Golf, where she uses her coaching skills to support people in bringing forth their full potential in their golf game and in their lives as a whole. She works every day at some of the most beautiful golf courses and driving ranges in Southern California, doing what she loves to do. Both of these changes unfolded as the result of her inserting the intent to create the best year of her life. She looks back on the changes that have taken place so quickly and effortlessly with a combination of disbelief and immense gratitude. This is the inexplicable power of living inside a conscious intent.

If you take only this one step and do nothing else, you will unleash the power to change your life. The intent to live your best year yet will generate an energetic force that will pull you toward the results you desire. This intent holds the power to change the fallow soil of undirected energy into potent, fertile ground where you can plant the seeds of your desires and watch them blossom into reality.

To create the best year of your life, it is essential that you understand that you are being guided either by a conscious intent that you create on a daily basis or by an unconscious intent from your past. There is always an intent operating behind the scenes, whether you are aware of it or not. If you're like most people, you are probably unaware of the intent that is currently guiding your choices, actions, and behaviors. Your unconscious intent might be to make it through another day, to prove to your parents that you are good enough, to protect yourself from being hurt, or to not ruffle any feathers at work. Or it could be one of a million versions of any one of these. But make no mistake about it: There is a hidden intent directing your life right now. The intent you are using right now was probably created early in your life, before you began making conscious decisions. The good news is that for you to create a conscious intent, it's not even important that you ever know the intent that is currently guiding you. All you need to know is that if you aren't experiencing the life you want; if you aren't making the best possible choices for yourself on a daily basis; if you're bored, resigned, or struggling; if you're continually making the same mistakes over and over again—your intent is most likely old, out-of-date, and just not working for you. If you continue to allow your unconscious intent to direct your life, what you can expect is that this year will be a new version of your last.

To ensure your success, you will have to first insert your conscious intent and then revisit it on a daily basis. To install a new intent that will drive your every move takes commitment and perseverance. Studies show that it takes twenty-eight days to permanently change a behavior or habit, and I suspect that the same is true of inserting a new belief into your consciousness. You can't just say that you're committed to creating the best year of your life and expect it to stick. You have to make a conscious effort to allow this commitment to become part of your internal belief system. Just think how many times your mother or father told you to brush your teeth before you got into the habit of doing it every day without even thinking about it. You must be that diligent in the beginning of this process: make a commitment to consciously choose, as many times a day as you brush your teeth, to have the best year of your life. As much as you may like it to do so, this new intent won't insert itself. If you're anything like me, you might think you shouldn't have to work so hard to have a great life.

I know that I was pissed off for years when I realized that having an extraordinary life was not going to come naturally to me. For some reason I believed I was owed this great life, and the thought of having to do something to create it made me mad. So, instead of just acknowledging that life was different than what I thought it should be, I dug my heels into the ground and lived as a victim for more years that I care to admit. The unconscious intent that had guided me most of my life was to create as much drama as possible so that everyone would pay attention to me. Not only was this intent no longer cute; it wasn't getting me where I wanted to go. Then, one day, after being beaten up one too many times by the circumstances I had created, I realized that no one was coming to save me. It was glaringly obvious that my entire existence was organized around my upsets and misfortunes. Even my friends were chosen for their ability to commiserate with my pain. So I stood at this turning point and realized that I had an important choice to make about the way I lived my life. I could remain angry at the way the universe and the human experience were designed and continue down the path that was leading me nowhere, or I could consciously create the absolute best life that was available to me. I'm happy to say that I chose to go for my best life.

My conscious intent to create the best year of my life and go beyond what I believe is possible for myself guides my every move, even to this day. It motivates me, lifts me out of the smallness of my own human drama, and drives me to make empowering choices for myself. My intent supports me in always looking for ways to make my life and the lives of others better. Instead of rebelling and whining ("Poor me! Why doesn't it come easy to me?"), I revisit, on a daily basis, my conscious intent and allow *it* to be my guide. Do I mind doing this? Not anymore, because my intent has paid off for me more times than I can remember. It has delivered me a life beyond what I thought was possible. And I know that if you are willing to do the work to ensure that your intent to have the best year of your life is firmly rooted in your consciousness, the same results will come to you.

Your intent will become even more powerful when it is openly declared to the world. If you're truly committed to your intent, all those around you will know it. I once heard Dianne Collins, creator of the QuantumThink program, say, "Your intent should pour out of you. It should emanate from every cell of your being, so that you attract the people and circumstances that can support you in manifesting your desires." In the simplest terms your intent informs your behaviors, actions, choices, and words. It becomes your personal operating system. To have the best year of your life, all you have to do is commit, right now, to the intent to create and experience your best year. Then each day for the next 365 days, wake up, remember your intent, and recommit to creating a year beyond what you think is possible. I promise you that you have the power to create it.

Do It! Create a Powerful Intent

Take at least three minutes at the beginning and end of each day to close your eyes and affirm, *"This is the best year of my life."* Remind yourself of this intent by posting visual reminders—such as notes and signs— in every room of your home and office. You can send e-mail messages to yourself each day, or attach a note to your phone so that every time you use it you will be reminded to take a moment to recommit to your intent. Make it known to the people who matter most to you that you are choosing to make this a year that surpasses all others.

TWO

Exposing
the Fantasy

*I*t's important that we understand that the best year of our lives is something we have the power and ability to actually attain. It's a vision of ourselves at our highest, not some far-out fantasy life that we will never reach. Living in fantasy—in hoping, wishing, and wanting—is a diversion that prevents us from being able to see clearly and stay on the path of action that can actually lead us to our best life.

Most of us have been trained to continually strive for the next thing, and the next and the next. However, if we deprive ourselves of happiness along the way, if we convince ourselves that our joy exists only at our desired destination, we become caught in an endless cycle of wanting and waiting, and waiting and wanting. When we are waiting for "one day" to come in order to be happy—to experience joy, fun, passion, or success—we are living in an illusion that deadens our spirits and robs us of our ability to enjoy our lives right now. There is nothing wrong with future thinking or goal setting. In fact, I believe that these actions are imperative if we are to reach our full potential. But living in the fantasy of "one day . . ." keeps our real lives—the ones you and I are actually living—on hold.

Fantasies come in every flavor and are often disguised as goals. They might sound like:

"When I finally get_____."

"As soon as I accomplish_____."

"When my husband finally_____."

"When my kids are old enough to take care of themselves, I will be able to_____."

"As soon as this_____ period is over, I will diet /get in shape / take care of myself."

"Next year I will_____, and *then* I'll be able to have the best year of my life."

This way of thinking leaves us resentful, resigned, and perpetually dissatisfied. Living in fantasy is sometimes referred to as *magical thinking,* because it really would be magic if by living in fantasy we reached our goals and utopia was actually there. We must understand that happiness, contentment, and peace are not stagnant emotions. They come and go and are always accessible to us. So if we wait for a particular outcome to occur in order to be happy, we will miss out on our right to have a life we love right now.

Many of us use our fantasies as a way to distract ourselves from what is actually happening in our lives. In the words of one unknown author, we develop a wishbone where our backbone should be. Our fantasies prevent us from taking action and making the changes that are necessary to better our lives. Our fantasies are tricky. Most of us don't even realize we have fantasies, much less that we are living in them. We are blinded by the ways they deceive us year after year, leaving us paralyzed, unable to make the changes we desire. If we insist on continuing to live in fantasy, we will more than likely wind up being one of those "should have been," "might have been," "would have been," or "could have been" stories.

To have the best year of our lives, we must expose the fantasy that keeps us waiting and wishing for things to change. Only then will we unlock the power to make our actual lives great. So I ask you to take a good look, and see what you are waiting for. What "one day . . ." fantasy keeps postponing your happiness and fulfillment to some distant time in the future? Do any of these scenarios sound familiar?

I'll be happy when I . . .

make a certain amount of money.
buy a house.
have a balanced life.
meet my soul mate.
finish school.
get my life under control.
reach my ideal body weight.

get the recognition I deserve.

send my children off to college.

have a baby.

find a new job.

have more time to play golf.

get a promotion.

have more sex.

find my true love.

am assured of my spouse's success.

have a fabulous new wardrobe.

get out of debt.

If any of these sound familiar, you are probably caught up in a fantasy that will deprive you of the joy and success you deserve.

When we step out of our fantasies and into reality 100 percent of the time, we take back the power we've placed in the future and receive the gift of seeing through clear eyes. Only by living in reality 100 percent of the time do we have the power to take action, make lasting changes, and become the masters of our lives. The late philosopher Earl Nightingale, a motivational speaker and author, once said, "Successful people are dreamers who have found a dream too exciting, too important, to remain in the realm of fantasy. Day by day, hour by hour, they toil in the service of their dream until they can see it with their eyes and touch it with their hands." Only when we are standing in reality are we able to take powerful actions that will lead us to an inspiring life. By breaking free of our delusions and fantasies, we become truly accountable for our destiny.

To move beyond your fantasies and actually *create* the life you've been dreaming about, you must uncover what it is you are truly chasing and how you think you will feel when you finally catch it. It's so easy to believe that some outside event will bring you the joy you're seeking. But what if you uncovered a greater truth? What if you found out—or remembered, because most of you already know this—that what you are actually chasing is not a particular goal or result but rather a particular *feeling*. What if you discovered that what you are craving is not the outside goodie—the new career, the fit body, the loving family—but the feeling that you think you'll experience when you get it?

You might think you will be happy when you finally find the perfect life partner, but I challenge you to look deeper. What are you hoping to feel once you find that person? Will you feel loved, nurtured, cared for? Will you feel safe? Secure? Validated or whole? I want to suggest to you that these feelings are what you're really chasing; and you think this imaginary person will bring them to you. If you're longing for fame, I want to suggest that it's not the fame itself you are seeking; rather, it's the feeling you think the fame will give you. If you ask yourself, "How will I feel when I become wildly famous?" you will discover what you are truly looking for. Maybe it's a feeling of worth or power, or a sense of importance or being special. Whether your fantasy is to own a home or to write a book or to make a million dollars, you want to ask yourself the same question: "How do I think I will feel once my goal is attained?" The answer to this question will reveal what you are really chasing through your fantasy.

We are all chasing the good feelings we hope will come from our external accomplishments. But the truth is, most often our accomplishments do not provide us with the joy we had hoped for, or if they do, the joy is short-lived. My own experience of this truth came as quite a surprise and sent me off into weeks of depression at a time when I should have been enjoying the amazing life I had created. A few months after my first book, *The Dark Side of the Light Chasers,* hit number one on the *New York Times* best-seller list, I found myself sad and confused. I wasn't sure what had hit me, especially since everything that was happening around me was all good. I began to examine my life and all that had happened over the past few months, and this is what I discovered.

For two years I had traveled over fifty thousand miles pro-moting my book, doing radio and TV interviews, lecturing at expos and bookstores, leading seminars, and helping thousands of people. My belief was that God had given me this work to help others and it was my job to do whatever it took to help those who wanted or needed it. Although the work was very rewarding and I was certain that I was doing the right thing, I exhausted myself day in and day out trying to get my work known in the world. My fantasy, of course, was that one day that would happen and then I could slow down, get some rest, and spend more time with my son and family. Well, here I was—my dream had become a reality—and I was more exhausted than before and devastated because the fantasy that success would make my life easier was now shattered.

The reality of my life was that now more people wanted me. More people had questions, requests, and needs, and I had to step powerfully into the present moment to be able to deal with it. Ultimately I realized that what I had been chasing for so many years was feeling important and knowing that my life mattered. If I had known earlier what my real desire was, I could have stopped every day and taken stock of my accomplishments. I could have taken an extra minute to digest the acknowledgments that people were always trying to give me. I could have read more of the mail that people were sending me as they shared the changes they had made as a result of reading my book. I could have closed my eyes once a day and asked God if my life mattered, or, even more simply, I could have called my sister Arielle, my mother, my brother, Aunt Pearl, or any other member of my family and asked them if I was important to them.

Any of these things would have allowed me to see that I was important and my life did matter. I could have given to myself what I had traveled the world chasing. And, in fact, that's exactly what I ultimately had to do.

I offer this story because I know so many people who think that if only they had more success, more money, more fame, more *something,* they would find happiness. It's just not true. It's a fantasy, an illusion that will trick you, if you let it, into giving up all the pleasure of the moment for some empty promise of the future. Don't be fooled. Don't bite the hook. I did, and I can tell you it was heartbreaking. It also cost me the joy of what should have been one of the best times of my life. The good news is, by dissecting your fantasy you can shortcut this entire process and reclaim the power to give yourself unlimited amounts of joy and peace. You simply have to distinguish your fantasy and identify the feelings you think you will experience once it is fulfilled. Then all you need to ask yourself is "What can I do right now to feel that way?" And be generous enough to give it to yourself.

Fantasy blinds us from right action and prevents us from seeing what we could do to improve our lives.

When we are living in fantasy, we can't see what is truly possible for ourselves. When fantasy is no longer an option, when we have both feet firmly rooted in reality, we begin to look for ways to improve our lives that were previously hidden by the illusion of "one day it's all going to work out." Lizbeth is a great example of this.

Even though she worked full-time as a personal trainer, Lizbeth fantasized about the day she would walk down the red carpet and be treated like a rock star. The funny but also sad reality is that Lizbeth can't even sing! Still, she was convinced that being famous would make her feel adored and admired. After realizing the cost of her fantasy—which had truly robbed her of experiencing the joy of her life—Lizbeth decided to stop working so hard to gain the adoration of others and to spend time each day admiring and adoring herself. Instead of wasting her time thinking about being someone she wasn't, Lizbeth began looking for ways to express her talents as a trainer. With the intent to live her best year yet, she told friends and colleagues that she was looking for bigger opportunities in her field. Just months after committing to giving up her fantasy life and creating a life rooted in reality, Lizbeth was asked to develop and star in a Pilates video, which, without her even trying, has given her the attention and adoration she was seeking. Her career has taken off, and she is awed by her own success. By busting her fantasy, Lizbeth unleashed the power she needed to create an exciting, rock-star life in a profession where she could shine.

Right now there are many actions that each of us can take to give ourselves exactly what we are chasing in the outer world. All we have to do is identify our fantasy and confess to ourselves that we are waiting for something to happen in the outer world to make us happy and fill us up. Then we can ask ourselves, "What is the feeling I would receive if that happened?" Once we uncover the feeling we are chasing, we can begin the life-changing process of giving it to ourselves. When we commit to taking care of our own needs and feeding ourselves the feelings we desire, the true miracle occurs and we find that everything we've been looking for is right within our reach. It does not exist as some far-out fantasy but as a reality we can claim if we are willing to do the work and be responsible for our own needs.

We've all heard it: Happiness is an inside job. It's true. By exposing your fantasy, you will once and for all dispel the myth that happiness, joy, and contentment live anywhere but within you.

Do It! Expose Your Fantasy

Write down a description of the fantasy life you are hoping and wishing you will "one day" lead. Dissect your fantasy to determine how you hope you will feel once that fantasy comes true. Then identify one action you can take each day to generate within yourself the feelings you are chasing. Commit to being 100 percent responsible for creating the feelings you desire.

THREE

Stepping into Greatness

*T*o experience the thrill of your highest expression and transcend the life you are living right now, to create a year beyond what is currently imaginable, you will have to create and commit to a vision that demands that you be the biggest, best "you" that you can possibly be. When you are deeply rooted in a clear, strong, and compelling vision for your best self, you will experience a level of joy and celebration that you probably haven't felt in years.

A strong, clear vision of who you are at your best holds the power to transcend your current reality, by-passing the day-to-day problems that might be keeping you stuck where you are. An inspiring vision will act as a force that lifts you out of the drama and predictability of your daily life and supports you in making extraordinary choices that will deliver you a life beyond your wildest dreams. Vision and passion are two sides of the same coin. One does not exist without the other. When you are firmly rooted in a strong vision for your future, you will have not only passion, but also the stamina to go out and get what you want in life.

Imagine yourself a year from today feeling that you are at the top of your game, knowing that you're moving ahead, achieving your long-awaited goals, and becoming the person you've always wanted to be. What could possibly be better than this? The journey to having the best year of your life entails that you look back into your past and recall the highest vision you've ever held for yourself and recommit to being all that you can be.

Even when our lives are great, there will be certain areas where we want to be more self-expressed, where we want to achieve greater success, where we long to be more than we are right now. Most of us are too busy to tend to these areas, so we put them off. But in order for us to have this year stand out from the rest, we must seek out those areas where we are falling short of our own expectations and commit to taking the steps that will lead us to the fulfillment of all of our potential. There is no better time to do this than right now.

In my late teens and early twenties, I wandered around aimlessly, wanting to be someone I wasn't. Even during the times when I was successful or was being praised for my accomplishments, I still ached for something more. I wanted the "new, improved" version of Debbie Ford. I hungered for fame, recognition, and importance even though I was doing nothing at all to earn them. I longed to stand out from the crowd, even when I was acting like everyone else. I yearned to be someone who was special, someone who would be remembered for their contribution to the world, even as I was drowning in my own self-absorption.

My desire to be someone I wasn't turned out to be both a blessing and a curse. The blessing was that I was never content or complacent in my mediocrity, and the curse was that I was horribly mean to myself, constantly berating myself for not being better than I was. Then one day I heard my mother telling her friend Vicki, who was always getting herself into messes, that she could be anything she wanted to be. Even though my mother had always touted the same message to me, somehow I couldn't comprehend that I also held this potential until that moment. But on that hot summer Florida day, standing in the kitchen of our house on 46th Avenue, something inside my head clicked: If Vicki could be anything she wanted to be, the same must be true for me. All of a sudden I realized that the visions of myself that peeked through my day-to-day reality from time to time might, in fact, be possible. That day on 46th Avenue marked the beginning of my quest to become the person I had always wanted to be.

My journey was long and arduous. But it was also mind expanding and exciting. What I discovered along the way, something that both excites and inspires me, is that each of us has the ability to find and nurture new parts of ourselves and become the people we aspire to be.

I became fascinated by the words of the writer and philosopher Charles DuBois, who said, "The important thing is this: to be able at any moment to sacrifice what we are for what we could become." After literally months of deep contemplation it finally dawned on me that Charles DuBois was in fact saying exactly what my mother had said. I was once again aware of the fact that each of us has a choice to stay stuck in the persona we have created or to let it go and allow a new expression of ourselves to emerge.

To this day, I remain awestruck by the fact that human beings are capable of this type of metamorphosis. We don't have to stay stuck displaying the same personality traits over the course of our lifetime but are free to transform into higher expressions of ourselves. Today I can honestly say that I know beyond the shadow of a doubt that human beings are capable of making radical and lasting change. After a decade of coaching individuals and leading groups, I have discovered that if I don't buy into people's perceptions of who they are and what they are capable of, I can bypass their public personas and see who they are in their highest expression. With a little effort, I can see their magnificence and their potential no matter what they look like or what condition their emotional, spiritual, or financial world is in. I can see through their acts, their personas, their fears and insecurities. I can see who they are apart from the baggage they carry around. The undeniable fact is that underneath all of our public personas, we already are that which we desire to be. Our only job is to see past our own limitations so that we can return to that which we already are.

Now, you might be saying that you like who you are—that you don't want a "new, improved" version of yourself. But as you know, all living things must grow or they die. It's part of your nature to want to grow and evolve. It's your soul's desire to want to break free from the limitations you've set for yourself. And this process of seeing beyond your limitations allows you to break free from who you've known yourself to be. Now, I ask, would it be worth your effort if one year from now you were able to look at who you are, what you've accomplished, how you're feeling, and declare, "Wow, I love who I am, I love what I've accomplished, and I love how I feel."? This is the experience that you create when you commit to evolving into the next highest expression of yourself. And you have the power to do this. It is a choice you can make that will radically shift the way you see yourself, others, and the world.

In order to have the best year of your life, you must keep opening up to greater realities and be willing to develop new aspects. If you insist on clinging to who you are right now, you'll miss the extraordinary opportunity to meet the next greatest version of yourself.

You can discover what that expression looks like by asking yourself, "What do I want the people around me to think about me? What do I want to be written about me when I die?" Then look to see if you embody a pure expression of those qualities that you want attributed to you. Next you can look to the outer tasks that you want to accomplish this year and ask yourself, "What kind of person could easily accomplish this? What qualities would they possess?" When you receive your answer, you will get a glimpse of the you that is yearning to come forth. Herein lies the formula for discovering the person you want to be.

Think about an area of your life where you want to improve or create something new and ask yourself,

"What qualities would I need to develop in order to achieve this vision?" If your deepest desire is to create a balanced life that includes time for family, fun, work, and play, you need to ask yourself, "What kind of person could effortlessly create such a life? Could a relaxed person create it? A disciplined person? Someone with clear priorities and strong boundaries?" If your vision is to be in optimum health, you would ask yourself, "What kind of person could easily create this?" You might see that it's a person who chooses wisely. If you then look deeper and ask yourself, "What kind of person would choose wisely?" you might hear, "Somebody who values life and respects their body." Or you might discover that someone who is committed or focused on themselves could easily accomplish that goal. Each of us will have a different response to this question. By identifying the qualities you will need to develop in order to manifest your vision, and taking the actions necessary to cultivate them, you will find the path to the best year of your life laid out clearly in front of you. Here is how it works.

Years ago, Cliff, one of my trainers, wanted to become a great facilitator. He asked himself what kind of person could facilitate groups with ease, and the answer he received was "Someone who is spontaneous in their communication and confident in themselves." *Spontaneous* and *confident* were the qualities Cliff would need to develop in order to reach his goal of being a great facilitator. I asked Cliff what actions he could take to nurture and develop those two qualities. To his own surprise, the thought that immediately came to mind was to take an improvisation class; this was the first time that idea had ever come up. Cliff saw that in taking such a class he would develop both his confidence and his spontaneity. He enrolled in weekly classes at a local college, and within a very short time these qualities, which were once lying dormant within him, were now accessible to him and provided just the skills he needed to fulfill his vision. In less than a year Cliff experienced a side of himself he never knew existed. And as he suspected, his spontaneous and confident aspects held the key to his becoming everything he desired to be.

After struggling for years with indebtedness and overspending, Danielle, my friend of ten years, wanted to have integrity in the area of her finances. When I asked her what kind of person would manage their finances with integrity, she said, "Someone who is responsible and diligent." *Responsible* and *diligent* were the qualities Danielle would need to develop in order to achieve her vision. She looked to see what actions or practices would support her in becoming responsible and diligent about her financial affairs. Several action steps immediately came to mind. She developed a relationship with a mentor—someone who handled her own financial affairs with integrity—and had weekly conversations with her. She paid off her credit cards and made a plan to restore her credit. She hired a bookkeeper to make sure all her bills were paid on time and arranged to have a certain percentage of her salary withheld to ensure that money was saved. Today, Danielle tells me with certainty that she is responsible and diligent with her finances. In this area of her life she has become the person she always wanted to be, and the joy of fulfilling her vision continues to guide her to creating the best year of her life.

Fulfilling your vision for the best year of your life and becoming the person you always desired to be is no more difficult than what I have described here. All that is required is for you to bring forth parts of yourself that you have not previously had access to. You do this by first identifying who you would have to be—what qualities you would have to demonstrate—in order to fulfill your vision and inspire yourself. Then simply take the actions that will support you in developing those qualities.

Imagine that each of the qualities that you desire to bring forth is a starving part of you that needs to be fed and well nourished in order to thrive. If you feed these parts with your attention, and make a conscious choice to express them, they will flourish. For example, if knowing that you are truly competent would support you in fulfilling your vision of the best year of your life, then every time you succeed in tasks that you normally don't do—and acknowledge those successes to yourself—you strengthen this aspect of yourself and move closer to your desired goal. If you nurture this hidden quality often enough, before you know it you will demonstrate competence in every area of your life. On the other hand, every time you make a choice that leaves you feeling incompetent, you are starving the competent part of yourself and moving in the opposite direction, away from your goal. What's important to remember is that for this process to work, you must keep the quality you're seeking in your awareness at all times, or it will slip back into obscurity. When your daily actions nurture the qualities that you want to bring forth, you will find that you are naturally being guided in the direction you want to go. If you want to bring forth responsibility, every time you make a responsible choice, every time you take a moment to question your irresponsible actions, you are making a choice in the right direction.

Another way of finding the qualities that will lead you to your best year is to identify the qualities that you believe were your nemesis last year, those aspects of yourself that got in the way of achieving your goals or that robbed you of feeling good about yourself. Whatever quality drove you last year—whether it was fear, laziness, procrastination, martyrdom, mistrust, or greed—making a conscious choice to develop the polar opposite of that quality will support you in making this a great year. If you think your insecurity got in your way, pick confidence as the quality you will feed and nurture on a daily basis. If your anger interfered in your relationships with people, see what the opposite of anger is for you. Maybe it's compassion, kindness, or empathy. Commit yourself to taking just one action a day to nurture this quality, and within weeks you will discover that you are making different choices, achieving different results, and creating a life that is consistent with the person you desire to be rather than the person you have been in the past.

This exciting process allows you to take the power of creating your best life into your own hands. Never again will you look at someone whom you admire and say, "I wish I had their strength, or their courage, or their charisma." Instead, you can choose to develop those qualities within yourself. It's important that you understand that the qualities you long to experience or see in another already exist within you. Think about it like a cloud covering the sun. Even though for the moment you can't see the sunlight or feel its warmth, you know the sun exists. If you wait long enough, the cloud will pass over and you will be able to see the sun again. The same is true of every quality you want to possess or express. Those qualities all exist within you, often hidden by a cloud of denial or covered by some behavior or a belief that you are not that. If you find and commit to embodying and integrating these hidden treasures, you will, as the great poet Rumi once wrote, "become the idol of yourself" and effortlessly achieve that which you desire.

Your vision for yourself this year should light you up, turn you on, and inspire you to bring forth the very best of yourself. Its job is to return the sparkle to your eyes and passion to your everyday experiences. Take a moment and consider a vision for yourself that would excite, move, and inspire you to claim each day, week, and month of this year as the best yet. What would have to happen over the next twelve months to make you want to stand up at the end of the year and shout, "Wow, my life is awesome! I want another year like that!"? Who would you have to be to create that?

Do It! Step into Greatness

Reflect on your vision for what would make this the best year of your life and then ask yourself, "What kind of person could effortlessly achieve this vision?" Identify two qualities that you will need to cultivate within yourself in order to manifest your vision with ease. Look to see what actions or daily practices will nurture the two qualities you have identified. What can you do on a daily, weekly, and monthly basis to let these qualities shine in full force in your life? For more support, download a worksheet at www.bestyearofyourlife.com.

Plan It

Spectacular achievements are always
preceded by painstaking preparation.

—ROGER STAUBACH,
NFL HALL OF FAME QUARTERBACK

FOUR

A Clean Slate

*E*very great achievement begins with a plan. But before you set out on the task of planning the best year of your life, you first must look back on the years that have come before and examine all of the obstacles that remain in your path. Think of this process as preparation—as cleaning the slate. We all know that if you don't fertilize the soil before you plant a garden, nothing can grow. If you don't knock down the old house and haul away the debris, it's impossible to lay a new foundation and build a new home. We have all heard it said a thousand times before: You have to get rid of the old to make room for the new.

There is nothing more important for each of us to do on a daily, weekly, monthly, or yearly basis than to bring closure to the events of our past and completion to all of our outstanding tasks. After all my years of coaching people to create successful lives, there is one thing I can say for sure: if somebody doesn't have a life they love, if the patterns of their past keep showing up, if they are continually distracted from the actions that would move them forward, all you have to do is look closely and you will find a pile of incompletions. However, if they are willing to go into their past and bring closure to those incompletions, they will easily be able to change the course of their lives and head in the direction they desire.

Closure is the doorway from the past to the future. It helps us create the strong and solid foundation upon which we can build an inspiring future. To bring closure to our past, we must be complete with every incident, project, or person with whom we've been involved. We cannot create a new, extraordinary life on top of a past that is riddled with incomplete projects, failed relationships, broken agreements, and unresolved issues. If we try to move forward without first completing the past, we may as well resign ourselves to the fact that we will continue to create more of the same.

Most of us are unaware of the extreme resignation that is brewing just beneath the surface of our consciousness. The voice of resignation is a little different for each of us, but its tone usually sounds something like this: "Why bother? It's never going to happen. I don't have what it takes. It's too much work. I don't have time. I can't deal with it. I don't deserve it." When we fall short where we had hoped to succeed, when our day-to-day lives fail to resemble our visions of what is possible, when our goals haven't turned into reality, our hope for a great life begins to die, our senses deaden, and gradually we become resigned about our futures. Since most of us are unaware of this fact or don't know how to deal with it, we wind up spending countless hours and much of our attention trying to cover up our resignation and fill the void that exists inside of us. Instead of making peace with our past, we develop addictions, create drama, and attract upsetting incidents in order to change our focus and avoid the painful feelings of not having expressed our potential. Resignation comes in many forms. It might show up as cynicism, sarcasm, or hopelessness. It can feel like depression, sadness, loneliness, or emptiness. Left unexamined, our resignation will continue to mask the real issues at hand while diverting us from fulfilling our highest visions for our lives.

For us to dismantle our resignation and open up to the possibility of an exciting future, we must first take a short journey into our past, and be willing to uncover the ways we've deceived or disappointed ourselves and others. We must see how we've sabotaged ourselves and our efforts to move forward, and admit to all the times we've been unclear, unfocused, or undisciplined. We must look at what traumas and emotional wounds we are still dragging around with us from the past and be willing to finally let them go.

Most of us try to forget about our mistakes, regrets, and misfortunes without bringing closure to them. But closure is a vital step that can't be missed if we are truly looking to leave the past behind us, where it belongs. We must understand that if we were meant to drag the past around with us each day it would be called the present rather than the past. Most of us are well aware of this fact, but for some reason we feel so attached to what happened yesterday that we have a hard time letting it go. Maybe it's because we long for some resolution—in the form of restitution, an apology, or a different outcome—and so, instead of letting go and moving on, we choose to hold on to our grudges rather than give up on what we believe we are owed. The problem with this approach, of course, is that if we need another person to participate in our closure, there is a good chance we will never get it. We can't count on anyone else to give us closure. We must claim it, demand it, and give it to ourselves. If it happens that someone from our past comes along and gives us what we've been waiting for, that's fantastic, but if we are to be 100 percent accountable for our lives, we must find a way of giving closure to ourselves so that we can move on. Closure supports us in healing our past and making peace with ourselves.

Closure is synonymous with freedom. It is easy to see this just by observing young children who haven't yet experienced a lot of trauma in their lives. If you watch a young child, you will see a smiling, jumping, joyful expression of a human being. You will notice they can get mad but can just as easily let go of their anger after they have expressed themselves. Most children can easily let go of yesterday and experience today unencumbered. Most of the time they can't even remember the upsets they experienced the day before, because there is no buildup; getting upset and getting over it are just a part of life. But if you observe children who have lived through many traumatic experiences, you will see their past reflected in their face. Their eyes will have lost some of the natural sparkle that we see in healthy children, and they will carry a certain heaviness with them. If you upset them, they won't be able to let it go as fast as a child who has never been traumatized. And if they don't find some way to work through the incidents from their past that have hurt them, it is likely that they will carry the pain of these events with them into the future. The same is true for all of us.

Holding on to our past could be compared to collecting newspapers from five, ten, twenty, or thirty years ago. Would you consciously choose to reread and rehash each upsetting story, or carry around the newspaper it was printed in, every day? Would you move the papers with you from place to place, from job to job, and from relationship to relationship? Would you take them on vacations and on special evenings out with friends? Even though most of us aren't consciously aware that we are carrying our upsets, resentments, and regrets with us each day, leaving the events of our past to fester without bringing them to closure robs us of our energy and drains our resources as surely as toting a stack of old newspapers around. To move forward, it is imperative that we recognize what we are carrying with us and be willing to let it go. We must make a commitment to finding closure.

If we don't bring closure to the upsetting incidents that have occurred, but instead harbor resentment, regret, or guilt, we can be certain that what's unfinished from the past will seep into our future and more than likely destroy our best-laid plans. How does this happen? It works like this: When we harbor negative emotions such as resentment, regret, and guilt, we become stuck in the negative energy that our unresolved experiences hold. We will then unconsciously be attracted to situations and people that display components of our unresolved past, arousing in us a visceral recognition of those unpleasant feelings. It's like in the movie *Groundhog Day*, where the lead character had to experience the same bad day over and over again until he finally shifted his perspective, changed his attitude, let go of his resentments, and allowed it all to turn out right. Our unconscious creation of similar unwanted experiences is nature's way of trying to give us opportunities to rectify, heal, make peace with, or complete what has been left undone. Only when we do the work necessary to become emotionally finished with our past can we remove the energetic roadblocks that stand in our path. Working with a clean slate, we are able to effortlessly draft a plan called our greatest life.

UNFINISHED BUSINESS

Physical incompletions—like clutter, half-completed projects, uncompleted to-do lists, and unfinished business of all kinds—prevent us from having a clean slate on which to create what we want. They weigh us down physically, spiritually, emotionally, and mentally, robbing us of our passion and joy for life. They are evidenced in our outer world as old files, extra pounds, clothes that don't fit, garages packed full of boxes, and equipment that no longer works or serves any purpose. When our lives are riddled with incompletions—whether we are consciously aware of them or not—our energy and mental focus are scattered, we feel resigned about our state of affairs, and we put off the projects and tasks that are truly important. If we are to create a powerful new future unlike our past, our incompletions must be purged so we can see clearly and move forward powerfully.

Think of each of your incompletions as little bloodsuckers. Imagine they are somewhere in your body, draining your self-esteem, your feelings of worthiness, your drive, your passion, and your confidence. If you could see each of these little bloodsuckers, wouldn't you quickly do what ever it takes to remove them? You would be horrified if you knew they were there, silently robbing you of contentment and peace of mind. Not for a minute do I think you would stand idly by and allow these bloodsuckers to feed off you. I know this is not a very pleasant image, but this is what's happening, whether you want to admit it or not. Bringing completion to all of your projects and your past affairs is a way to rid yourself of these hidden parasites that drain your energy and cloud your vision. Completion is a gift that you give yourself. It gives you permission to put the past in order, to put everything in its place, to leave it whole and complete.

I am reminded of Tony, one of my coaches, who had been struggling for years to get his new business off the ground. It seemed no matter how hard he worked, or how much he believed in the services he offered, he could barely make ends meet. One day I casually asked Tony what unresolved issue from his past might be preventing him from succeeding in his present endeavor. He told me he had failed in business before: Years earlier, after convincing his friends and family to invest in a start-up company, his business had gone under and all his investors had lost their money. Although Tony had quickly regrouped and moved on, he had never offered an apology to those who had invested their money and lost it. Tony began to recognize how the lack of closure regarding this incident had been haunting him, undermining his confidence and his feelings of worthiness. Realizing he was bringing his past into the present, Tony made a list of all the people he needed to apologize to and courageously made amends to each of them. In the months that followed, Tony and his business were infused with new life, and Tony went on to make his business a success. This is what happens when we make peace with the past.

When you have closed the book on your past, you will experience a sense of deep satisfaction. As you begin to liberate the powerful energy that has been locked within your unfinished business, you will naturally have the desire and the willingness to create a life beyond what you have known. You can move forward with energy, excitement, and a fresh perspective. It is in the state of closure that a new vision for your future will arise: You will see with newfound clarity exactly what is possible for you. By bringing completion to the past, you become ready to move on to the future.

In order to have the best year of our lives, a year that completely surpasses our current reality, we must clean out the old and make room for the new. We can't plant a new crop on top of last year's and expect it to grow. In order to till the soil of our consciousness, to prepare it so that something new can grow, we have to clear away the deadwood. Closing the door on our past lays the foundation for a bright new future and allows new doors to open before us. It leaves us deeply rooted in our personal integrity and powerfully grounds us in the present moment.

Do It! Create a Clean Slate

Make a list of the unresolved projects, tasks, and relationships that are keeping you tied to the past and blocking you from expressing your greatest self. Identify the actions you will need to take to bring closure to each incomplete issue from your past. Imagine how good it will feel to have a clean slate on which to create the best year of your life.

FIVE

Avoiding Your "No-Cookie Zones"

*O*n the journey to the best year of our lives, there will be obstacles: There will be disheartening dead ends; there will be distracting temptations, luring us off the road to our dreams. To ensure that this will be our finest year yet, we will have to learn how to avoid these pitfalls, which have prevented us from moving forward in the past. We will have to steer clear of the habitual patterns and behaviors that offer us no rewards—the thoughts, habits, excuses, and behaviors that keep us from living our best lives. I call these alluring byways *no-cookie zones,* because if we stray down these familiar paths, we will wind up no closer to our dreams than where we are right now. These behaviors are the easy way out. They often feel like the shortest path to a solution or to gratification—but, as you will soon realize, they lead us nowhere and offer us no rewards. In other words, there are no cookies at the end of these tempting paths!

Many years ago, I came across a wonderful and insightful little poem by Portia Nelson, contained in her book *There's a hole in my sidewalk,* which illustrates beautifully how our no-cookie zones keep us engaging in the same behaviors over and over again. It goes like this:

CHAPTER 1
I walk down the street.
There is a deep hole in the sidewalk.
I fall in.
I am lost . . . I am helpless.
It isn't my fault.
It takes me forever to find a way out.

CHAPTER 2

I walk down the same street.

There is a deep hole in the sidewalk.

I pretend I don't see it.

I fall in again.

I can't believe I am in the same place.

But, it isn't my fault.

It still takes a long time to get out.

CHAPTER 3

I walk down the same street.

There is a deep hole in the sidewalk.

I see it is there.

I still fall in . . . it's a habit.

My eyes are open.

I know where I am.

It is my fault.

I get out immediately.

CHAPTER 4

I walk down the same street.

There is a deep hole in the sidewalk.

I walk around it.

CHAPTER 5

I walk down another street.

No-cookie zones—or NCZs, as I like to call them—are like Portia Nelson's hole in the sidewalk. They are often disguised as harmless little choices: eating a donut on day three of your diet; buying four new CDs when you could be paying off your credit-card debt; gossiping to a co-worker when you could be spending your time making the project you're working on fantastic; putting off paying your bills even though you know you'll be slammed with late fees. Although they take different forms for each of us, our NCZs act like termites, eating away at the very foundation of our greatest life.

NCZs are potholes in the road to the best year of our lives. Even when we're consciously aware of them, our NCZs hold a certain power over us. They draw us in even after we have declared that we won't fall into the same hole again. NCZs rob of us of our self-esteem and confidence and sap the vital energy we need to actually create our best lives. When we spend our precious energy exploring paths that lead us nowhere, we can expect nothing more from our lives than what we already have. Our NCZs bind us to mediocrity and guarantee that we will remain stuck right where we are.

Most of us lie to ourselves about the destructiveness of some of our behaviors. This is because our most self-sabotaging behaviors are usually wrapped in deep denial. We deny the consequences of our actions and fool ourselves into believing we will get what we want even as we continue down the same fruitless path. Our denial tells us, "I can get away with this one more time"; "No one will know"; "I don't need to deal with this now"; or "I don't really care if I get that thing I've been after anyway."

You know you're in an NCZ when you have the realization that you've been down the road you're on enough times to know you're going in the wrong direction. You are aware of the fruitlessness of the chase even while you're going through the motions. You can usually identify an NCZ because you have sworn off that particular behavior one too many times to believe yourself. An NCZ might be as harmless as expecting your teenager to take out the garbage without your asking, or it could take the form of drinking that second glass of wine at dinner. It might look like waiting until the last minute to renew your driver's license or making yourself late for a meeting because you tried to get one more item on your to-do list done. No matter how big or small it is, if it takes away from you feeling great about your life, it's time to give it up.

Sarah, a mother of two young boys, yearned to feel calm, peaceful, and confident. However, stress, anxiety, and uneasiness were the emotions she experienced most of the time. When I gave Sarah the assignment of observing her daily NCZs, those behaviors that rob her of confidence and peace of mind, she discovered something she had never seen before: The act of multitasking—which she thought was making her more efficient—was actually robbing her of the feelings she was longing for. I asked Sarah to write down each of the self-defeating behaviors she engaged in, and to make note of what each one cost her in terms of peace of mind. Here is her list.

> 1. I talk on the phone while shopping for groceries and supplies, which leaves me feeling

distracted and anxious. It ends up costing me time because I usually have to call the person back to complete our conversation, or return to the store for items I've forgotten.

2. I complete things that I need to do so quickly that afterward I wonder if I've actually done them or not and I have to go back and check my own work. This leaves me feeling discouraged and insecure about myself.

3. I try to complete business calls while picking my children up from school. If they try to share about their day while I am on the phone, I am often short and impatient with them. Although in the moment I am convinced that I need to get one more thing done, I always regret my behavior later on.

A look at Sarah's list makes it clear that her NCZs are taking her life in the opposite direction from where she wants it to go.

I've spent many years wondering why, in spite of people's deep desire for change, they continually make the same disempowering choices that prevent them from realizing their goals and desires. After years of coaching thousands of great people, I have come to understand that we continue to visit our NCZs because at some level we are afraid to change. We're scared to grow up or afraid of failure. Most of us would rather stay where we are, even if we complain about it, than go for the gold and fail. So we keep falling into the proverbial hole that we know so well as a way to ensure that we will stay where there is some familiar comfort. Although we might claim that we want better, more productive, more fulfilling lives, we continue to hold on to what isn't working. We use one excuse after another as to why we don't have the life we desire and why our dreams have not turned into reality.

Often, the NCZs that blind us the most are the ones we engage in every day. We may not even notice them because they have become so ingrained in our daily behaviors. In order to reclaim our power to choose in the areas where we have blindly followed our base impulses, we must identify the choices, behaviors, thoughts, excuses, and beliefs that keep landing us in the same predicaments. Although they might seem immediately gratifying, there is ultimately no reward for us in these behaviors. By labeling these choices NCZs, we bring more awareness to the consequences of our actions. Then, when we find ourselves about to enter an NCZ, we can make another, more powerful choice, the same way we would if we encountered a Road Closed sign while driving.

NO-COOKIE ZONE NO. 1:
EXCUSES

Excuses are perhaps the biggest NCZs of all, because they will never get us where we want to go. They are a dead end. Excuses prevent us from being responsible and keep us from standing in our power. They leave us feeling powerless and victimized by our circumstances. They're an invitation to blame—to point our fingers at someone other than ourselves. *To excuse* by definition means "to regard with indulgence; to view leniently or to overlook; to pardon." So I ask you, what would happen if you couldn't use even one excuse this year? What if, as part of your commitment to creating the best year of your life, you chose to give up even your favorite and most justified excuses? What if no one was accountable for how this year turned out except you? As you may know, there is an endless list of excuses as to why you can't or won't or shouldn't make this the best year of your life.

Excuses are automatic; they take no thinking or creativity. For many of us, we are so familiar with our excuses that we don't even realize they are excuses. They show up as the truth of our lives. But hear this: Excuses are not the truth. We all have them, we all use them, and we all pretend we are made powerless by them. But if we are to have the best year of our lives, we have to be willing to give up *all* the excuses we've used. We have to ask ourselves this fundamental question: "Do I want to align with the greatest vision of myself, or do I want to align with my excuses?"

Excuses keep us from taking responsibility for our lives and prevent us from seeing the truth about our current reality. They are literally our attempt to "excuse" ourselves from acting like the responsible, powerful, creative human beings we are. Excuses have become a socially acceptable way of giving ourselves the "out" we might be looking for. Our excuses scream, "It's not my fault"; "I couldn't help it"; "I didn't have time"; "My kids needed me"; "I told Sally to handle it"; "That's not in my job description"; "I can't do it all"; "It's too big"; "I'm too stressed out"; "It's too much work"; "I'm too busy already"; "I'm not smart enough"; "I did my part, but they didn't do theirs"; "People around me are irresponsible"; "Someone else should handle this"; "Everything will fall apart if I don't do it"; "I have a headache"; "The system is screwed up." Excuses transfer all of our inner power to outer circumstances and strip away our ability to create results. They sabotage our dreams for our future and send us, time and time again, down the familiar path of our past. Excuses have the ability to infiltrate our deepest desires and best-laid plans and rob of us of having a life we love.

One of the participants in a class I led on creating the best year of your life came to one of our follow-up meetings with what was for her a mind-blowing realization: Her excuses were justified—that is, they had credibility. She was stunned. But when I had her look deeper, she could see that *all* excuses are justified. If we couldn't justify them, we wouldn't use them. We would just come out and say, "Hey, I am going to use an excuse now not to do, be, or have what I want in my life." Most of us have a lot of proof that our excuses are real. Of course, some of our excuses are easier to justify than others—for example, "I can't expand my business because I have small children at home"; "I can't get out of debt because my husband or wife won't participate"; "I can't buy a new computer and begin writing my book because I don't have any money in the bank." On the surface, these appear to be more than excuses. They show up as the truth, because there is evidence to prove the limitation for which we are arguing. But on closer examination, if we are willing to look beyond our "I can't," we will see that unless there is some circumstance that makes it physically impossible for us to do what we say we want to do, it is a form of an excuse—an "I won't." Even if it's justified, it's still an excuse.

How do I know this? Because if it were a matter of life or death, most of us could figure out how to earn enough money to buy the computer, how to raise our kids while growing our business, or how to get out of debt without the help of our spouse. Now, we might have to give something up in order to accomplish our task. We may have to sacrifice some of our free time or we might have to find the courage to ask someone for help. We might need to take responsibility for educating ourselves rather than looking for support from our partners. The point is, if we are truly committed to reaching our destination, we must give up all of our excuses, justified or not. Then and only then will we be the masters of our own destiny.

We have all heard countless stories of people who have taken their lives into their own hands and created unpredictable results. These are people who came from nothing—without education, without support, without resources, without advantages—and who have gone out into the world and made their lives extraordinary. These are people who ignored their circumstances and defied the odds. They just made things happen, without excuse. Every one of us has this powerful ability.

If you are to live a life beyond your wildest dreams—creating successes you never believed possible—you must take on this level of responsibility. If you make your life an "excuse-free zone," you will move much more quickly through whatever obstacles are in your way and produce a thousand times more results than you are now seeing. All excuses are NCZs that will prevent you from having the life you desire. Today is your opportunity to commit to the high road and lead an excuse-free life. When there are no excuses, there will be only one path for you to take: the path to the best year of your life.

Do It! Identify Your Excuses

Make a list of the excuses you use to justify the condition of your life. Make the powerful choice to give up even your favorite, most justified excuse for why you can't have the best year of your life. Notice how much more effective you are when you align with your vision rather than your excuses.

NO-COOKIE ZONE NO. 2: NEGATIVE INTERNAL DIALOGUE

One of the nastiest and most debilitating NCZs comes not in the form of an outer obstacle, but from our own minds. When left unchecked, our negative internal dialogue can wreak havoc in our lives, interfere with our best-laid plans, and prevent us from reaching—or even going after—our goals. Our thoughts dictate our behaviors and our actions. Our minds tell us what we are and are not capable of doing and achieving. Most of us try desperately to manage our minds, or better yet, to ignore or resist the continuous negative chatter that plays over and over. But we must address our internal negative dialogue if we are to succeed in creating a life beyond the boundaries of what we know.

What I find tremendously fascinating is that most of us think our negative internal dialogue is the truth. We fail to understand that we all have it and that, although it is there, we don't have to listen to it. To the extent that we believe our internal dialogue, we will continue to believe our self-imposed limitations and stay within the confines we have built for ourselves. In order to enjoy a life that is beyond, better than, and more fulfilling than the life we are living today, we have to come to terms with our internal dialogue and take back the power we have given to it.

Once we distinguish the internal dialogues that keep us stuck repeating the same old behaviors and listening to the same old instructions, we can highlight them and label them as NCZs. Then, instead of listening to them and following their marching orders, we can say, "Aha! I'm being visited by an NCZ, and just for the moment I am choosing not to follow it." Bringing awareness to our thoughts before taking action gives us access to making a better choice—one that might actually lead us down the path of our dreams.

Another way our internal dialogue sets us up to fail is by way of our negative expectations. We *expect* that we won't get what we want, that people won't like us, or that we are going to experience pain or failure. Our negative expectations are not the truth, but some of us live as though they are. Often our stress and anxiety is caused not by the actual events of our lives but by anticipating a negative outcome. Even when circumstances occur that prove our expectations wrong, we are often left in a state of upset that prevents us from feeling gratitude for the positive outcome that did occur.

Negative expectations take us out of the present moment and launch us into a distorted projection of the future. They prevent us from experiencing or even noticing the good that exists in every situation. The moment we create a negative expectation, we place the people and circumstances of our lives inside a box labeled No Good Can Come from This. Our negative expectations separate us from reality. They stop us from knowing the facts or asking for the facts. And perhaps worst of all, our negative expectations become self-fulfilling prophecies, drawing to us the very experiences we are trying to avoid.

The best way to diminish the power of our negative expectations is to acknowledge the times they didn't come true. A participant in one of my coaching programs did this recently. She was invited to a party where she was sure she wouldn't fit in. Her internal dialogue, riddled with negative expectations, told her, "You're not going to have fun. People won't like you." But, sticking to her commitment to having the best year of her life and to making every moment extraordinary, she created a new expectation—to have fun—and was pleasantly surprised when she had the time of her life. Reality had busted her negative expectation wide open! By taking the time to consciously acknowledge that her negative expectations were not always the truth, she was able to recognize those expectations as an NCZ and create positive expectations that would deliver her the best year of her life.

It's a great exercise for you to look at how much time and energy you invest in the NCZ of your negative internal dialogue, and how much of your internal conversation sets up your negative expectations. Then, because you have the right and the ability to do so, stop and identify this dialogue as an NCZ and make a new, powerful choice that is in direct alignment with creating the best year of your life.

Do It!
Take Note of Your
Negative Internal Dialogue

Begin to notice the negative internal dialogue that saps your energy and undermines your self-esteem. The next time you begin to hear its familiar chatter, distinguish it as a no-cookie zone instead of blindly following its instructions. Become aware of your negative expectations and practice replacing them with positive expectations.

NO-COOKIE ZONE NO. 3:
THE BLAME GAME

The rules of this game are as follows: It's not my fault, it's your fault. I didn't do it, and I am going to make you suffer even if I have to destroy my life in the process. The game is to look for any person, place, or thing and make them responsible for what's going on (or not going on) in your life. It's a game where nobody wins. It's a game where you keep bumping up against the same walls as you struggle to find someone who is the cause of your discomfort and discontent.

For twelve years, my friend Laura blamed her husband because he didn't provide her with the lifestyle that she believed a man should give her. Instead of focusing on her own career and pursuing ways that she could make more money to buy the possessions that she wanted, she wasted years of her time and energy blaming her husband for her unhappiness. When she finally realized she was trapped in an NCZ called the Blame Game, she decided to reclaim her power and take all that energy she had squandered on making her husband wrong and put it toward her career. Catching herself in this NCZ empowered her to get on with her life and her dreams.

To have the best year of our lives, we are going to have to stop blaming others for the condition of our lives. To the extent that we blame others for any circumstance, even if we believe it to be their fault, we diminish our power to make the changes we are craving to make. Blaming has become the disease of our time. It sets us up to be victims, which then renders us powerless over our circumstances. When we are feeling stressed, drained, or resigned, we can be certain that we have fallen into victim consciousness and made another person responsible for our reality. Anything we say, think, or do that points to someone else renders us powerless.

Once you realize you are living as a victim in any area of your life, the next step is simple: Notice who you are blaming, and then stop it. Claim responsibility for your own experience. No matter what another has done to you, if you continue to blame them, you will, unfortunately, lose the game. Even if you were taught to hold on—to cling—to your grudges, I urge you to give them up now. If you don't, you will have no other option than to drag the past into the future and continue down paths that lead you somewhere other than where you really want to go. Creating the best year of your life requires you to stand tall, accept 100 percent responsibility for yourself, and move forward, regardless of what others are or aren't doing. The Blame Game is always an NCZ, because there are definitely no goodies at the end of that tunnel.

Do It!
Stop Playing the Blame Game

Identify where in your life you are blaming someone else for your circumstances and allow yourself to see how much more power you would have if you took 100 percent responsibility for making this the best year of your life.

NO-COOKIE ZONE NO. 4:
RIGHTEOUS POSITIONS

Our righteous positions should be considered NCZs because they are the devils that transform us from passionate, youthful, flexible individuals into bitter, tired, resigned, inflexible human beings. Our righteous positions are often created without our conscious awareness. We have an experience early in our lives, and out of this experience we form a conclusion. Because we don't want to admit that our conclusions are unfounded, flawed, or limited, we argue for them. And in so doing, without even realizing it, we adopt a righteous position that can interfere with our journey toward our best year. Because most of us despise the thought of admitting we are wrong, we often cling to our righteous positions, even when they make us miserable or prevent us from having a life that we love. Zack is a good example of this.

Zack is a talented young man who once worked for Beth, a colleague of mine. He made a great deal of money doing work that he found fulfilling. In the beginning they worked as a team, but over time it became impossible for Beth to work with Zack because he was always arguing with her about the way she wanted to run her business. They spent many hours discussing their differences and trying to see if there was a way to make their situation amicable. But after a year or so Beth realized that she was arguing with a righteous position that had very little to do with her—a position that would ultimately cause Zack to walk away from a job he loved.

Upset by his inability to resolve his conflicts with Beth, Zack came to seek my council. In the course of our conversation, we discovered the source of Zack's righteous position. It turns out that years earlier, when he was just a boy, after several incidents of being abused by a female cousin, Zack made a decision that no woman would ever dominate or hurt him again. This decision, infused with righteousness, unconsciously became Zack's position. Even though he was aware of his position, he was unwilling to give it up. Eventually it became impossible for Beth and Zack to work together. This was clearly a case where a righteous position won out.

All righteous positions are birthed out of fear. If we are willing to find and face the fear, we can easily let go of the positions that keep us from seeing our situation clearly. If Zack had been willing to confront his fear of women hurting or dominating him, he could have diffused the power this position held over him and allowed another reality to emerge.

Our positions act as blinders that keep us repeating the patterns from our past. Here are some righteous positions that my friends, family, co-workers, and community members have shared with me over the years.

Rich people are greedy.
Women should be passive.
Men should pay for everything.
Everyone should graduate from college.
Death is bad.
Failing is bad.

Vegetarians are more spiritually evolved.

Good people are selfless.

Everyone should leave happy.

People should take better care of themselves.

Democrats are bleeding-heart liberals.

Republicans are big-business fascists who care
only about money.

People are idiots.

Parents should stay together for their children.

Mothers should be home with their kids.

Men have it easy.

I can do it better.

Divorce is bad.

Anger is bad.

Hate is bad.

Everyone should be in good shape.

Television is a waste of time.

It's too late to start a new career.

Poor people are lazy.

Rich people don't care about anyone but
themselves.

People shouldn't be judgmental.

People should want to help other people.
It's a dog-eat-dog world.
I have to take care of everybody.
No one is there for me.
I know what is right for me.
I don't need anybody.
I know better than the rest of the world.
I'm right and you're wrong.

In order to neutralize our positions, we must first admit that we have them! We must be willing to accept the fact that we are not God almighty and we do not know it all. To have the next year of our lives be ten times more inspiring, fulfilling, and exciting than the last, we will have to surrender our positions and be willing see things from a different perspective. We will have to lay down our righteousness and be wrong sometimes. We have to be willing to see life through new eyes and give ourselves and others a break. When we surrender our righteous positions, we return to what Buddhists call *beginner's mind*. This is the mind of an innocent child, where all realities are possible. Beginner's mind allows us to open up to new experiences and try on new perspectives. This state of mind is what is required to make every year of our lives the best yet.

Do It!
Identify Your Righteous Positions

Begin to notice all the places where you're sure that life is a particular way and make a list of the righteous positions you hold in that area. Ask yourself, "What am I afraid to find out if I let go of this righteous position? What new belief would better serve me in creating the best year of my life?"

NO-COOKIE ZONE NO. 5:
SELF-DEFEATING BEHAVIORS

If you long to get out of debt, then find yourself catalogue shopping in the middle of the night, you have entered an NCZ that threatens to rob you of the results you desire. If you crave more passion and intimacy with your spouse while fantasizing about another, more perfect lover, you are in an NCZ that does nothing to move you closer to your desired outcome. If your goal is to increase your income by 20 percent, staying in a job that has no growth potential is, for you, an NCZ. If you want to lose twenty pounds, nibbling on desserts filled with fat and sugar is an NCZ that will ensure that your goal remains at arm's length.

Any behavior you engage in that is self-sabotaging, that takes you away from what you want, or that distracts you from your goals is an NCZ. These behaviors sap your vitality, leaving you exhausted and without access to the powerful energy you need to create your best life. Let's look at a few examples of such behaviors.

- *Playing solitaire on the computer at work when you have ambitions of moving up the corporate ladder*

- *Prioritizing your to-do list and then starting at the bottom*

- *Stopping for fast food when you're committed to healthy eating*

- *Focusing on what other people need to do rather than on what you need to do*

- *Getting on the phone with an old friend right before you're supposed to be at the gym*

- *Saying no, no, no to your kids and fifteen minutes later giving in*

- *Saying that you want to lay off alcohol and then meeting a friend at a bar*

- *Longing to enhance your sex life and then staying up late every night watching TV*

- *Dreaming about putting away money for your future and then spending more than you make every month*

- *Saying you want to have a closer relationship with your teenage kids and then criticizing their choices*

- *Procrastinating taking actions that will give you what you desire*

- *Worrying about what other people think of you*

We must give up self-defeating behaviors like these if we are to make this the best year of our lives.

Rick, a participant in one of my advanced training sessions, discovered that his biggest NCZ was watching movies into the wee hours of the morning. He was at the height of his career when he took up this habit, and for almost two years he watched his business slowly suffer as he stumbled half asleep into his office in the morning.

Pauline, an emergency-room nurse, wanted nothing more than to have a close relationship with her husband and two sons, but every night when she got off work, instead of hanging out and doing homework with her kids she chose to leave it to her husband to watch over the kids while she shopped catalogues and surfed the Internet. I could go on and on, but I am sure by now you have probably identified one or more of your own NCZs.

We all have them, and most of us have sworn them off more times than we can count. But now, standing in the presence of our commitment to live the best year of our lives, we have the perfect incentive to make new choices. That is what living inside a powerful intent supports us in doing. What will determine whether this will be the best year of our lives or just another year that is lived and soon forgotten is the quality of the choices we make every day. We get to choose at every moment whether we are going to once again walk down the street with the hole in the sidewalk or choose a new road altogether. Allowing our excuses, negative expectations, unconstructive internal dialogue, and self-sabotaging behaviors to dictate our choices is about the most ordinary choice we could make. If we are willing to begin making a series of extraordinary choices now, we can turn the possibility of living our best life into our predominant reality. All we need to do is begin by making a few such choices each day.

Do It!
Identify Your
Self-Defeating Behaviors

Make a list of the behaviors, choices, and habits you engage in that are in direct opposition to the fulfillment of becoming the person you desire to be. Now consider what new behaviors and choices you can make to have this year be extraordinary. Please visit www.bestyearofyourlife.com to download a worksheet for identifying your NCZs.

SIX

Planning Your Year

*I*t was 4 A.M. and I had been up for about an hour, unable to fall back to sleep. At first I just thought I had woken up for a few moments like I do every night around 3 A.M., but twenty minutes later I realized that this was more than my usual restlessness. My mind began to think over all that had happened during the day, and my peaceful slumber quickly turned into a state of unrest. I tried to understand what I was so uneasy about. What was concerning me so much that I couldn't fall back to sleep? Then I heard these words: *"You don't have a plan."* My immediate thought was "Of course I have a plan. I have so many plans. That must be the problem, too many plans. . . ." As my mind continued to race, I struggled to make out the exact meaning of the words in my head. Then I got it. I realized that I had spent the morning with Gary, my fiancé, and the contractor who was to begin building our home the following week. There were at least a hundred details that would need my attention over the next few months, and I had no plan as to when or how I would get through it all. Since, as usual, I already had a schedule that would be daunting to even the most avid overdoer, my psyche was awakening me to the fact that I was setting myself up for nine months of stress. And this was just a little middle-of-the-night sample of what was to come if I didn't put a plan in place.

Now, I have to admit that this news came as quite a surprise to me, because I would be the first to insist that I have a plan for everything. I coach people all day long on their plans. But, lying there at 3:40 A.M., I could see that although I had a well-thought-out plan for most areas of my life, I did not have one for what would be one of the biggest projects I would undertake all year. I realized I had set sail on a tremendous journey . . . with no map. I knew where I wanted to go, but I had no idea what it would take to get there. It hit me that if I didn't take the time to construct a well-laid-out plan, complete with time lines and budgets, I would be embarking on a very long, sleepless journey through construction hell.

Well-conceived plans are the key to peace of mind. If we want to rest peacefully, day or night, we must chart our course carefully and know what and where and how we are going to make our visions a reality. Even though our plans might change, having a strategy in place allows us to change our course and adjust our time lines without causing ourselves unnecessary anxiety. I've been lucky in my own life, because I have somewhat mastered the game of manifesting what I want without having to do so much actual planning on paper. But I could see that in this case, the cost of "winging it" was greater than I was willing to bear, especially with the fate of my dream home at stake. I couldn't afford, either financially or emotionally, not to know the precise actions I needed to take each day. So I got out of bed and began putting down on paper everything I needed to get done so I could rest assured that everything would get done in the proper time, with impeccable integrity.

While I was writing, I discovered several key questions that I would need to answer in order to design a specific plan that would ensure that I reached my goal. Although answering these questions required some time and effort on my part, I knew that the time I invested in planning would save me stress, anxiety, and regret later on. Following are the questions I asked myself, along with my responses to them.

1. Where do I want to go? What is my vision or final destination?

   My destination is to create a dream home together with Gary, a home for our family to live in, where we can feel warm, cozy, serene, and well nourished.

2. What is the specific goal that will move me toward my vision? And by what date do I want it to be complete?

   My home will be complete and ready to move into nine months from now.

3. What is the exact scope of the project or vision?

I have to pick out floors, cabinets, sinks, bathtubs, shower hardware, kitchen cabinets, kitchen counter, door hardware, and furniture for the living room, dining room, family room, office, and bedrooms.

4. What are the important milestones along the way?

I want to have everything picked out in the next six months, including all the furniture.

5. What skills do I already have that will support me in achieving my goal?

— *I am decisive and know what I like.*

— *I have a clear vision of the end result.*

— *I am good at delegating.*

6. What skills will I need to develop to get the job done?

   — *I will need to trust my gut instincts.*
   — *I will have to develop the discipline to stick to my plan and stay within my budget.*

7. What assistance or support do I need?

   I need a list from the contractor outlining everything that needs to be picked out and by when.

8. How much of my time will be required on a daily or weekly basis?

   I will need to devote six hours a week for approximately ten weeks, then two hours a week for the remainder of the project.

9. How will I schedule this time in my calendar?

   I will devote an hour a day to assess where we are, make phone calls, and check in with the contractor to make sure we are on schedule and that the contractor and his crew have everything they need from us to do a fantastic job.

10. What are the No-Cookie Zones that I need to watch out for?

   – *Not following the time line*
   – *Scheduling appointments throughout the week rather than consolidating them into one day*
   – *Making rush decisions that I will later regret*
   – *Letting others sway my gut instincts about the type of look I want*
   – *Using the excuses: "It can wait until next week"; "My work is more important than this"; "I don't have time so I will let others make the choice for me"*
   – *Handing my power over to others who I believe know more than I do*
   – *Not taking total and complete responsibility for the final result*

- *Insisting on a particular product, fabric, or manufacturer*
- *Going over our budget on items that are not crucial to the finished product*

11. Whom will I ask to hold me accountable for keeping my word?

   Gary.

12. What are the consequences of not following my plan?

   - *Feeling stressed out for the next nine months*
   - *Not having the house completed on time*
   - *Not being able to move in by our target date*
   - *Going over budget and not having enough money to finish the job*
   - *Having restless, sleepless nights*
   - *Getting sick because I haven't had proper rest*
   - *Not being able to enjoy my awesome life*

— *Feeling resentful and angry because I haven't done what I said I was going to do*

— *Having unnecessary tension and conflict with Gary*

— *Stripping myself of the joy and excitement of building a dream home*

13. What are the rewards for following my plan and reaching my destination?

— *A beautiful home where our family can live, love, and thrive*

— *An inspiring place that Gary and I can come home to every day to get recharged and nourished*

— *A beautiful space where our friends and family can come to hang out, be fed, and feel the warmth and love that lives in our hearts*

The moment I put my plan on paper, I felt grounded and safe. All the concerns that were racing through my head and the free-floating anxiety that was robbing me of peace subsided. Even though I didn't have all the answers I needed in order to accomplish my plan with ease, grace, and joy, I had it all laid out in front of me in the form of a clear, step-by-step action plan. Instead of feeling overwhelmed and anxious, I now felt calm, clear, and assured that I could move forward powerfully.

When you know where you are going and how to proceed, you are gifted with the power of certainty. Having certainty about your life provides you with a sense of peace and supports you in making clear and exact decisions. Then when you wake up in the morning you can consult your plan instead of your emotions or your chattering mind. Following an action plan allows you to see what there is for you to do each day to get where you want to go. When you are clear and certain, you will be empowered to move forward with clear, concise actions that will deliver you swiftly to your desired destination. Certainty is a state of being that calls forth right action.

Fulfilling your vision for the best year of your life requires thought and introspection. You wouldn't set off on the best vacation of your life without taking some time to consider where you want to go, how you're going to get there, how you want to feel, how long you want to be gone, whom you want to go with, what you want to take with you, and what guides or support you might need along the way. Having the best year of your life is really not much different than planning an awesome vacation. It takes time, discussion, planning, decision making, and an array of other skills. To create it, you will need to pinpoint exactly what changes you will need to make in order to consider this your most extraordinary year and what structures you need to put into place. You will also need to know what it will take to sustain your vision, to keep it in your awareness, so that six months down the road you won't forget where you are going. Without a clear structure in place to support you in making the shifts you are committed to making, it is unlikely that you will be able to execute them. Your vision must be laid out in a plan of action right in front of you, step-by-step, if you hope to actually arrive at your desired destination. A strong plan of action will yield you quantum results and will ensure that you don't fall into the familiar patterns of your past. It will support you in steering clear of the holes in the road and help you avoid your NCZs. You must commit yourself to your plan and use it as your guide if you are determined to reach your destination. In the sections that follow, I will lead you through the steps you will need to take in order to bring your vision for the best year of your life to fruition.

DEFINING YOUR GOALS

One of the effects of our desire-driven, achievement-oriented culture is that there seems to be a lot of confusion around what a goal really is. Most of us have taken some class or read a book or an article on goal setting. Many people that I coach claim they have goals that they're working on, but upon closer scrutiny they discover that they are actually holding a vision or entertaining a fantasy instead. What they want is not clearly defined, so there can be no way for them to tell if they ever achieve it. More important, they have no specific plan in place to ensure that they're taking the consistent, productive actions necessary for achieving it.

If a vision is the big picture of how we want our lives to be, then the process of setting goals and milestones is specifying the pathways that will take us from the seeds of our desires to the fulfillment of our visions. Setting goals and breaking them down into milestones, which are markers to track our progress, is a clear and effective process for productive change.

Although the practice of setting goals and specifying clear milestones may seem like a rather pedestrian and tedious chore in the more glamorous conversation of living the life of your dreams, in reality it is the most important piece. You can think of this process as the drawings and plans for constructing exactly what you most want. You wouldn't try to construct the home of your dreams without plans. So why would you believe that it's possible to construct the life of your dreams without them?

Goals, together with well-designed and carefully executed action steps to support them, provide one of the most amazing things available in our lives—a reliable method for getting where we want to go. It's truly an exciting and empowering adventure as you face and move beyond your current limitations. Think of it: What could be more thrilling than looking back on your year and recognizing that you've made significant strides toward your vision while becoming more of the person you've always wanted to be?

To be truly useful and effective, our goals must have certain characteristics and meet a few crucial tests. Without goals that have these characteristics, we are either relying on the whims of fate to bring us what we want or fooling ourselves into believing we're making progress in our lives when we're really just standing still. Let's look at each of these characteristics.

- *First, a goal must be* specifically defined. *This means that you must state exactly what it is you want to achieve, in a way that is clear, concise, and easily understandable.*

- *Next, a goal must be* measurable. *You must be able to objectively quantify it in such a way that it will be unmistakable when you've achieved it.*

- *Third, a goal must be set up within a* time line. *You need to set a specific time to start and a date by which you will achieve it.*

■ *A goal must be* realistic. *There must be a high probability that you can actually achieve it.*

■ *You must have the ability to achieve the goal* within your control. *It must not require any particular good luck or divine intervention or depend upon another person for it to be fulfilled.*

■ *Your goal must have a plan for its accomplishment—a clear structure that includes the specific step-by-step actions, resources, skills, and supports necessary for its achievement.*

Let me give you an example of a goal that is specific, measurable, realistic, and has a plan for its accomplishment.

KELLY'S GOAL: to lose twenty-five pounds and return to her ideal body weight

HOW WILL I KNOW WHEN IT'S ACCOMPLISHED? I will weigh 130 pounds and wear a loose-fitting size eight.

WHEN WILL I START WORKING ON THIS GOAL, AND BY WHEN DO I WISH TO ACHIEVE IT? I will begin on February 1 and accomplish my goal by August 1.

WHAT IS MY PLAN FOR ACCOMPLISHING THIS GOAL?

1. On February 1, I will hire a coach to support me in creating food plans and keeping my word.

2. I will eliminate sugar, alcohol, and most dairy products from my diet.

3. I will eat only when I am physically hungry, and I will not eat while I am working or emotionally upset.

4. I will cook my own meals at least five times a week.

5. I will exercise five times a week, for at least one hour a day.

I encourage you to pick goals that, when accomplished, will render you unstoppable and unrecognizable, even to yourself. It's imperative to prioritize your goals. You want to avoid the pitfall of having so many projects on your plate that you fail to get any of them done. Pick the two that will give you the greatest sense of having lived an extraordinary year. Accomplishing two goals that are important to you will support you in building the self-confidence to fulfill all your other objectives.

We must be motivated to work on our goals and invest our time and energy in them. Whereas our visions need to inspire and evoke strong good feelings, goals don't necessarily need to do either. Often the goal itself may inspire and produce positive emotions, but frequently the motivation comes simply from the knowledge that the pursuit of our goal is leading us, step-by-step, toward the fulfillment of our vision. As Henry David Thoreau once said, "If you have built castles in the air, your work need not be lost; that is where they should be. Now put the foundations under them."

Do It! Define Your Best-Year Goals

Identify two goals that you could set for yourself that will support you in creating your vision and becoming the person you want to be. Write these goals out on a piece of paper, making sure they are realistic, measurable, and specific. Consider the skills and resources you already possess that will support you in accomplishing these goals, and those that you will need to develop or acquire. Go to www.bestyearofyourlife.com to download a worksheet to guide you.

CREATING A STRUCTURE FOR SUCCESS

Once you have distinguished your goals and created a time line specifying when they will be accomplished, you can begin to create the structures that will ensure your success. Structures are what allow us to work toward our goals effectively and achieve them consistently. A structure is defined as any system or support we put in place in the outside world to help us manage ourselves, our time, and our actions. Calendars and schedules are structures that help us manage our time. Action plans are structures that support us in realizing our visions. Coaches, trainers, buddies, and others who hold us accountable are structures that help us to manage and monitor our actions.

Although the concept of structure may seem mundane, boring, and even stifling, structures are actually exciting, because they help us accomplish what we say we want to do. How many times in your life have you had a great idea or inspiration, set out to do something that would make a huge difference for yourself, your family, or your community, and either started it and never finished it or never even took the first steps toward making it happen? Without structure it's highly unlikely that you'll ever fulfill your vision or achieve outstanding results. For those of you who avoid having structure in some part of your life, you might be feeling a little threatened or rebellious at the moment. Your resistance to structure might show up for you as tightness in your chest or a knot in the pit of your stomach, or as a desire to be free, unencumbered, and not tied down. But this is the time to confront the part of you that denies you the right to reach your goals. This is the time to tell the truth about how many of your previous goals have collapsed on the starting line.

A solid structure is what provides the tangible steps that lead us clearly and inevitably to the life of our dreams. The bigger the desire, the more important it is to have a well-designed, carefully written plan with time lines and specific action steps. This element of structure, more than any other, is what transforms desires into goals and dreams into reality.

Like a goal, a structure needs to be clearly defined, realistic, and usable, and it also needs to have room for flexibility and unexpected occurrences, like days when we're just feeling down. All of us will have days when we feel lazy or uninspired or just too tired to think about having the best year of our lives. Resignation will seep in and destroy our best-laid plans if we don't make room for disappointment, frustration, laziness, and resistance. These states of reality exist, and it's unlikely we will be able to avoid them.

So my suggestion is that you plan for these down days. Include them as part of your structure, and work them into your monthly schedule. Of course you will want to decide how many such days you are going to allow yourself, depending on what's going on in your life or what stage of your goal you are working on. Make a commitment to enjoy, or a least relax into, these unwelcome days. Just imagine how good it might feel to claim a "misery" day for yourself. If you don't want misery, you could claim a depressed day, a grumpy day, an ungrateful day, or an unproductive day. How much easier will it be to survive these down days if instead of beating yourself up for them you actually welcome them and give yourself complete and total permission to experience them? You might think that welcoming them is setting up a pattern to indulge yourself, but actually the complete opposite is true: When you surrender and welcome any emotion that is present within you, something magical happens and suddenly it has the ability to pass through you. It is only when you resist and fight against a mood or emotion, or think it shouldn't be there, that it gains power and the feelings intensify.

I would set a limit of three or four down days a month and start charting your moods. Your down days might just be a signal telling you that you need to make some more changes or set some stronger boundaries. Instead of fighting them, which usually doesn't work anyway, why not try listening to them and see where they might be guiding you? Without room to breathe, or the flexibility to accommodate change, a structure can overwhelm or suffocate you.

A good structure should feel supportive and nourishing. It should feel like a strong ally rather than a cruel taskmaster. One of the ways to avoid having your structure turn against you is to make sure you don't overplan or take on more than you can reasonably accomplish. That is why I'm suggesting that you take on only two goals for the year rather than four or five. If you attain these two goals before the year is up, you can take on two more. Overplanning is a sure setup for failure. Overplanning defeats the very purpose that it is designed to fulfill. It's so easy to get overly excited and want to take on all areas of your life, but creating the best year of your life requires you to set yourself up to win. And to do this, you must focus on what's truly important.

If you're still not sure if creating a structure to reach your desired goals is worth your time and energy, I would like to inspire you to action by sharing the following true account.

For four years, Nancy, one of my students, put off dealing with the tax debt she had incurred when she was in business for herself. Never taking the time to break the problem down into a manageable structure with actionable steps, she viewed her situation as a huge, insurmountable task that would never get resolved. The drain on her vitality, self-respect, and ultimately her wallet was enormous. Finally, after years of avoidance and denial, she set a goal to be free of her debt within twelve months. She then created a structure, milestones, and a specific plan to ensure that she stayed on track. She made the necessary appointments with her accountant and tax adviser and arranged to take the time off work to keep them. Because these appointments were on her schedule, she had a specific time line to keep her on track in gathering all the necessary figures and paperwork. Nancy enlisted the support of a friend, someone she admires who is great with money and savings, and asked her to hold her accountable for doing what she said she would do. Although it was an involved process, Nancy stayed true to her structure, followed her plan step-by-step, and within a period of three months she turned the entire situation around and constructed a payment plan that had her completely absolved of her debt within ten months. She now feels a sense of pride and accomplishment and has the confidence to go after her bigger dreams.

This is the promise of a solid structure. It is there to hold and support you and keep you focused during those times when you want to deviate. A structure will ensure that you stay on the straight line to success.

Do It!
Create a Structure
for Your Success

It's time to create a structure for the fulfillment of your goals. Allow it to be a creative and fun project. After all, you're creating the structure that will support you in living your best life. What could be more fun than that?! Use the questions on the following page as your guide, or visit www.bestyearofyourlife.com to download a worksheet that will direct you step-by-step through the process.

1. What is my vision?

2. What two goals will support me in moving toward my vision?

3. By when do I want to achieve these goals?

4. What is the exact scope of each goal? What is involved in their fulfillment?

5. What are the important milestones along the way to reaching these goals?

6. By when will I achieve these milestones?

7. What skills do I already have that will support me in reaching these goals?

8. What skills will I need to develop in order to reach these goals?

9. What assistance or support will I need?

10. How much of my time will be required on a daily or weekly basis?

11. How will I schedule this into my calendar?

12. What are the NCZs that I need to watch out for?

13. Whom will I ask to hold me accountable for keeping my word and staying on track?

14. What are the consequences of not following my plan?

15. What is the reward for following my plan and achieving my goals?

SEEING DISCIPLINE AS YOUR ALLY

Structure without discipline is, of course, useless. Putting together a well-constructed plan with all the structures in place and then ignoring it is like mapping out a road trip from New York City to San Diego and then, instead of keeping the map next to you so you will know where to go, folding the map up, putting it in the glove box, and never looking at it again; instead of following your plan, you just hop on whatever freeway looks appealing and live in the hope that one day you will wind up at your destination. I don't recommend this. I promise you it doesn't work. What each of us needs to cultivate in order to ensure our success is self-discipline. Discipline by definition means training that produces moral or mental improvement. Its job is to bring orderliness to our lives. In its highest form discipline has the ability to deliver us complete self-mastery. Discipline is the greatest gift we can give ourselves. It supports us in staying true to what's really important and making sure we achieve our goals.

But for some of us, the fear of discipline will be one of the biggest roadblocks we face on the path to the best year of our lives. Afraid that we will be constrained, confined, or controlled, many of us resist discipline at all costs. We allow the defiant seven-year-old inside of us to take the reins and operate our lives under the motto Nobody's Going to Tell Me What to Do. Yet what most of us don't realize is that our fear of discipline causes us to sell our souls and forfeit our dreams. We think of discipline as our jailer rather than our savior, constraining us rather than providing us with the ability to follow a specific action plan that will deliver us the results we desire.

We equate discipline with hard work and think of it as something that inhibits our right to be free.

You might be asking, Can we be too disciplined? The answer is yes. Of course, we can overdo anything. And if that is really your issue, you are welcome to skip ahead. But for most of us just the opposite is true. We might have discipline in the areas of our lives that work, but we lack discipline in those areas of our lives that most need our attention.

If we resist taking the actions we know we need to take, we will more than likely find ourselves distracted, cranky, and defensive. When we continue to put off the tasks that are right in front of us, we feel drained, tired, and lifeless. Yet most of us will put off what we could do today until tomorrow and continue to suffer the consequences. We will delay getting the job done or confronting the issues at hand so we can do whatever we feel like doing in the moment, hoping it will all turn out okay. But the cost of this behavior is steep. We put our plans on hold, our dreams on the back burner, and slip into the empty abyss of denial. It's a monotonous game. And—what's even more discouraging—it doesn't work.

If it did, we would each have all the things we say we want. But instead, we keep postponing our happiness, putting off until tomorrow all the things that are crying for our attention today.

Procrastination is the disease of our time. It is an energy-sucking, debilitating syndrome that robs us of our dreams, our self-respect, and our passion. And self-discipline is the only ticket out of this self-sabotaging pattern. Discipline can't be argued with. It can't be persuaded or manipulated. Discipline doesn't ask you if you feel like doing it. It doesn't even give you an option. The voice of discipline says, "This is the plan of action. I said I would do it, so I will." Discipline doesn't care what you think (sorry, it's not personal). It isn't the slightest bit interested in your excuses; it cares only about your success. We must cut into the illusion that not doing it today is an option. We must break free from any pattern of self-talk that wants to veer us away from following our structure and reaching our goals.

People are constantly whining to me, "But, Debbie, it's so hard." But it's not so hard. What's hard is living with yourself when you don't do what you say you are going to do. Doing the work, being disciplined, and having your goals mapped out in front of you is the easy road compared to saying you want something and not doing anything about it day after day. That's hard. It's hard on your self-esteem; it's hard on your morale; it's hard on your heart; and it's very hard on those around you. Just ask somebody who has paid the price of procrastination.

Cara used to cringe every time she entered the bedroom of her two young children. The sight of bulging toy boxes, overcrowded bookshelves, and closets filled with clothes they had long outgrown sent her into a state of overwhelm, regardless of what else was going on. Each time she saw the mound of stuff growing taller, she would tell herself she would get to it one day when she had more time. Cara even came to dread birthdays and other holidays, knowing that there was no space in either of her children's rooms for another book, toy, or any other gift. One day Cara decided that the cost of her procrastination was too much to bear. She marked the following Saturday on her calendar as "Kids' Room Clean-up Day." She then asked her husband to plan an all-day outing with their children so she wouldn't get distracted from her task. She made a list of everything she would need to complete the project, from storage boxes to extra hangers, and treated herself to a CD she'd been wanting in order to make the job a little more enjoyable. Cara spent that Saturday completely revamping her kids' rooms and found that at the end of the day she actually had more energy than when she started. Cara now knows she has the discipline to accomplish what she sets out to do, and this has translated into other areas of her life. This is what is available to all of us if we are willing to be disciplined and structured in our tasks.

It's easy to trick ourselves into believing that by not having a plan and structure we have more freedom. But actually, just the opposite is true. Until we translate our heart's desires into a specific action plan, and until we summon the discipline to stick to that plan, we remain prisoners of our own procrastination. Procrastination is the enemy of discipline. Self-discipline is truly the path to freedom.

Do It! See Discipline as Your Ally

Reflect on the ways you have resisted being disciplined, and calculate what your avoidance of discipline has cost you. Make a list of all your failed attempts at making something happen. Make a list of what will be available to you if you create a plan for the best year of your life and bring forth the self-discipline to stick to it.

TAKING ACTION

I once read a sign that said, "To reach our goals, we must at times run with the wind, at times against it. But certainly, we must never stand still." It all comes down to taking action. Action is the accelerator. Taking focused actions that move us toward our goals and visions could be compared to being inside a finely tuned sports car and stepping on the gas. When we take clear, deliberate actions, we feel the awesome thrill of aligning with our own desires. We experience a force unlike anything else that lifts our spirits and fuels our every move. The energy of being in action calls us to powerfully express the best of ourselves. It urges us to tap into untouched resources that lie dormant inside of us when we are lacking clear direction and idly passing the time. Right action allows us to see opportunities that were previously hidden and supports us moving powerfully toward the future we desire.

Writer W. M. Lewis said, "The tragedy of life is not that it ends so soon, but that we wait so long to begin it." So many of us have wasted so much of our vital energy talking about the great life we could have or will have or should have. All that is fine, but it will not deliver us the best year of our lives. It won't motivate us or anyone else, and it certainly won't give us the success and fulfillment we long for. Today we each get to choose how we will use the resources we hold. We each get to decide if the actions we take will move us powerfully forward or keep us stuck in the past. Having a desire and not taking the actions that will move us closer to what we long for is both disheartening and cruel. When unattended, our unfulfilled desires turn on us, and instead of bringing us excitement, passion, joy, fulfillment, and satisfaction, they steal our self-esteem, our courage, and our faith and fuel our resignation and dissatisfaction.

When we are taking action toward our desires, when our daily, monthly, and yearly behaviors are bringing us closer to achieving the goals we have set for ourselves, our desires become a source of inspiration and passion. Confident that we are on track to an inspiring future, we enjoy thinking and talking about our goals, knowing that we are on our way to fulfilling them. When we are in action, moving toward our dreams, we have the faith to move forward and create grander visions for our lives, allowing ourselves to set greater goals and achieve them. Our desires then act as fuel, inspiring and motivating us to step into a larger vision for ourselves.

Do It! Get into Action

Review the structure you created to keep you on track toward the fulfillment of your goals. If you haven't done so already, assign a specific date by which you will reach each of your important milestones. Identify the actions you will need to take this week to ensure that you meet your first milestone, and take them.

Live It

Don't ask yourself what the world needs.
Ask what makes you come alive.
Because what the world needs are
people who have come alive.

—HAROLD WHITMAN

SEVEN

Impeccable Integrity

How can we ensure that we will keep moving forward on the road to the best year of our lives, even on the days when we're tempted to veer off? What will support us in making sure that our daily actions are consistent with our vision for the best year of our lives? The simple answer is: living a life grounded in integrity.

Impeccable integrity is the foundation of a successful life. It is the support, the backbone, and the structure that enable us to bring forth our best effort and make daily choices that are in alignment with our deepest truth. When we are living inside our personal integrity, we are connected to our core, unwavering in our commitment, and worthy of our own trust. When we are acting with impeccable integrity, every area of our lives becomes a reflection of our highest vision and our deepest values. Our behaviors, actions, and choices are consistent with who we desire to be in the world. We cannot build a rich, rewarding life without having in place a firm foundation of impeccable integrity.

Many of us don't act in accordance with our personal integrity because we're afraid that the road of integrity won't bring us the love, money, security, and success we want. Maybe we believe that in order to succeed we have to project an image of success, so we choose to live beyond our means. Or we might think that we need to make a certain amount of money and that the honest route won't do it for us so we decide to cheat a bit. Or maybe, in the middle of a business deal, we fear that it might slip through our fingers so we exaggerate or lie in order to ensure our success. We may fear that we don't have enough of our own creativity, so we lay claim to ideas that are not our own. In these seemingly inconsequential acts, a vicious cycle begins. Our fears become the dictators of our actions, while our personal integrity gradually gets washed away. The cost of this behavior is huge. It takes us off the road to success and turns us down a long, winding track of struggle and stress. Every time we veer off the straight line of our personal integrity, every time we use an excuse to be something less than who we really are, we separate from our deepest truth and give up our right to success and fulfillment.

All over the world we are seeing the results of people selling out their integrity for money, success, and greed. On any given day, we can also see the cost of veering off the straight line of integrity to try to capture something that is not truly ours to begin with. Just as crime doesn't pay, neither do the crimes that we commit on our own lives. It's a crime to sell out our highest potential for a feel-good moment or a perceived gain that is clearly an illusion. Impeccable integrity will be the greatest ally we have if we only give it a chance. It will lift our spirits and instill in us an abundance of confidence and self-worth—all much-needed tools on the way to the best year of our lives.

When we are living in alignment with our personal integrity, we are in tune with all of our resources and instincts and are able to make powerful, life-enhancing choices that will lead us straight to success. We naturally operate from deep within ourselves and are in touch with our truth. This truth guides us to the exact ideas, people, and situations we need in order to create the success we desire.

On the contrary, when we are out of alignment with our personal integrity, we struggle constantly to find meaning and fulfillment. We get caught in the trap of trying to make our lives work out, instead of taking the actions that are aligned with our goals and desires. Let me give you an example.

My friend Derek is a bright, wise, well-educated man who left his home in England and came to live in the States when he was in his early twenties. Like his father and his two sisters, Derek has a talent for investments and real estate, but he chose early on to stay far away from the family business and pursue his own, to him more meaningful, career in the field of healing. When I met Derek fifteen years later he was still struggling to find work that he loved and to discover his true place in the world. As Derek and I got to know each

Integrity anchors naturally vary from person to person, depending on our respective goals, objectives, and vision. When we are untrue to our integrity, we feel insecure and ill at ease. We feel stress, struggle, and a gnawing feeling deep in our gut that something is not right. Without our integrity anchors to keep us on course, our fears, doubts, and critical voice rule our reality, undermining our serenity and peace of mind. If we fail to give ourselves the priceless gift of staying true to ourselves—to our values, morals, and integrity—success and happiness in all areas of our lives will elude us.

One of my good friends, Jenna, has a desire to create a fulfilling and nurturing family life. She knows that to achieve this goal she must feel like she is being a good mother to her three boys. There is nothing more important to Jenna than to know at the end of each day that her sons have had the experience of being totally loved by her. Jenna created three integrity anchors that will ensure her success in feeling like a great mom.

1. Each week I will plan one fun event with my boys where we can laugh, play, and connect.

2. Each week I will spend at least three hours at the gym working out so I can feel more energized when I am with my boys.

3. Each week I will schedule a half hour of quality time alone with each of my sons, going over homework or reading.

In the past, Jenna has gotten caught up in her career rather than honoring what's truly important to her. And each time she deviates from her integrity line and ignores what she knows is an essential practice for her, she finds herself unhappy and frustrated soon thereafter.

Each of us must create specific integrity anchors for the important areas of our lives. Paying our bills on time, spending time with our children, telling the truth, eating well, exercising, meditating, putting money away for our future, and volunteering at a favorite charity are all examples of integrity anchors that keep us in line with what's truly important. Imagine these anchors as pillars of strength that allow us to remain connected to our highest self and our innate wisdom.

By identifying your integrity anchors, you get a firm grasp on the actions, behaviors, and daily disciplines that are vital in order for you to succeed at living your best life. By staying true to your integrity anchors in each key area of your life, you gain the courage to ask for what you need. You open up to greater levels of self-esteem and worthiness. When your integrity is firmly intact, you are blessed with a deep faith that your needs will be met and your goals and desires will come to fruition. You gain the freedom to be utterly transparent and the courage to allow yourself to be seen, knowing that you have nothing to fear or to apologize for. Following your integrity anchors allows you to access all of your inner resources and become an inspiration to yourself and others. You will no longer need to have the outer world validate you, because you will naturally validate yourself. And most important, you will feel worthy enough to stay true to your intent to make this the best year of your life.

Do It!
Live with Impeccable Integrity

Recall your vision for the best year of your life. What do you want to accomplish, and how do you want to feel? Now create two integrity anchors that you can practice each day to ensure that you stay on track toward the fulfillment of your vision.

Keep your integrity anchors in your awareness and make them a part of your daily routine, knowing that following them will set you on the straight road to success.

EIGHT

Feeling Groovy

*H*aving coached and trained tens of thousands of people worldwide, I can tell you that feeling good about ourselves is the most essential prerequisite to living our best life. In our society, in which we are always looking outside ourselves for more, better, and different ways to feel good, we often neglect and minimize the importance of how we feel inside. But I would assert that having high self-esteem is our greatest ally. When we feel great about who we are, we radiate an undeniable magnetic energy that attracts to us all the things we desire. People we've been meaning to call magically show up in our lives. Ideas and next actions for our projects come easily. Our relationships with others—even those with whom we've had problems in the past—are more lighthearted and fun. When we are kind, generous, and respectful toward ourselves, we have the confidence to go out and get what we want in life. Feeling good about ourselves enables us to live a life of fulfillment, success, and satisfaction.

When we love and respect who we are, we naturally feel worthy enough to have it all. We are able to acknowledge that we are both perfect and imperfect, and we accept that we will at times be moody, fail in our tasks, and make mistakes. When our self-esteem is high, we acknowledge our accomplishments, think nourishing thoughts, and behave in ways that inspire self-respect. When we feel good about ourselves, we give up our unrealistic expectations and stay grounded in reality. We draw healthy boundaries and take on only what we are likely to accomplish. When we are being true to our intent and vision of who we aspire to be, we take the time to get clear about what we want and why we want it, and we create a plan and structure to make sure we don't get lost along the way. Feeling good about ourselves is vital if we want to stay young at heart, healthy in mind, and strong in spirit. Having high self-esteem unlocks our ability to express our full potential and gives us the confidence to go out and get what we want out of life.

As you probably know, it's easy to feel great about yourself when everything is going your way: Your bank account is full, people around you are treating you well, your career is soaring, your kids are happy, and the bills are paid. But the more difficult task is to accept yourself even in the presence of your flaws. Can you imagine having the ability to feel good about yourself even when you're feeling unworthy, insecure, or scared? Or holding yourself in such high regard that you treat yourself with compassion even when you're feeling angry or jealous? How fantastic would it be if you accepted yourself when you failed to meet your deadlines or show up for your kids' soccer practice?

As long as we feel shame, judgment, doubt, conflict, or embarrassment about who we are, success and contentment will elude us as we chase in the outer world the love and acknowledgment we haven't given to ourselves. One of the greatest spiritual truths I can share is that our outer world is a mirror of our inner world. At every moment our outer world reflects back to us the way we are feeling about ourselves. This means that the better we treat ourselves on the inside, the better people will treat us on the outside. This may seem astonishing, but chances are you've experienced it for yourself. Just think about a time when something bad was happening. Maybe you felt down because somebody left you or insulted you, or because you were violated in some way. Maybe it was a time when you didn't have enough money or lost a job. Think about the mood and the energy that were surrounding you then. You may have noticed that when you felt bad inside you seemed to attract people, situations, and experiences that reflected more of those bad feelings.

The same is true when we are feeling good about ourselves. Think about a time in your life when you were happy and excited about what was going on around you, a day when you felt fantastic. Or a time when everybody was supporting you and cheering you on, when you had everything you wanted, when you felt content and happy about your life. Maybe it was at the beginning of a new project or venture, or when you found out you were about to have a child, or when you met someone you felt could be the man or the woman of your dreams. Do you remember how great the world looked through your eyes that day? Can you remember how much nicer, kinder, and more accommodating people seemed?

All of us have had days where the world just seemed like a better place. But what we sometimes fail to realize is that we are the ones who created that experience. Because we were feeling great and optimistic, we radiated a positive energy into the world that attracted similar experiences to match our own. When we feel good about ourselves, we feel energized, inspired, and motivated. We see possibility where we once saw limitation. And I am here to remind you that this feeling is available to you at every moment, because the shift takes place within you. If you're going to continue to source your-self 365 days a year, you must realize that you are the one who holds the power to make yourself feel good, and that you do it by treating yourself the way you want to be treated. This means that if you want more acknowledgment, respect, love, or understanding, you must take the time to cultivate those feelings within yourself. I've already mentioned the phrase "Happiness is an inside job." And I'd like to suggest to you that everything you want—whether it's happiness, success, money, romance, or joy—is an inside job. And it begins with feeling good about yourself. When you make the commitment to honor and respect yourself, the entire world will open up to you.

So, you might be asking yourself, "What can I do to feel great about myself, to experience feeling groovy on the inside?" To begin, you must understand that every day you will have countless opportunities to make choices that will raise your self-esteem and make you feel better about yourself or that will diminish your sense of self-worth. Remembering your intent, staying in line with your vision, following your plan, and being disciplined in your integrity anchors are invaluable tools that will ensure feeling good about yourself. Setting measurable goals and doing what you say you are going to do are actions that build your self-esteem. Making the choice to nurture within you the qualities you admire in others will build your self-esteem. Appreciating what you have and what you've done is something you can do every day to feel great about yourself. Each of these actions will influence how you feel inside. All actions count. There are no free rides. Even the choices that no one will know about, the little ones you think won't be noticed, have the power and ability to change the way you feel about yourself, and hence how you feel about your life.

Think about it this way: if, twelve months from now, you knew at the deepest level just how worthy and deserving you are, if you had compassion and acceptance for your imperfections, if you took actions every day that moved you a little closer to your goals and desires and felt the pride of your own accomplishments . . . if twelve months from now you were the person you have always wanted to be—wouldn't you consider this to be a great year? Having the best year of our lives requires us to continually choose thoughts, behaviors, and actions that build our self-esteem. As you make the empowering choice to take actions that leave you feeling proud, you will be able to stand up with confidence and ask this great world to give you everything you deserve.

Do It! Start Feeling Groovy

Make an honest assessment of the behaviors, habits, and choices you make on a regular basis that diminish your self-image or cause you to feel bad about yourself. Remember that the best year of your life is built upon a foundation of high self-esteem. Set aside some time at the beginning of each day to reflect on the choices you can make and the actions you can take that will elevate your sense of worthiness and leave you feeling great about yourself. Commit to taking at least three actions a day that nourish your self-esteem.

NINE

Claiming the Moment

*I*n the past week of your life, you lived a total of 168 hours, more than ten thousand minutes. But how many of those ten thousand moments that you experienced were truly memorable? How many of them were significant enough that you'll remember them in a week, a month, a year, or five years from now? Will you remember any of those ten thousand moments for the rest of your life?

For most of us, the moments of our lives slip by unnoticed. We are so busy trying to survive and get everything on our to-do lists completed that we fail to realize that this moment is all we have. In the rush to get things done, we take the people in our lives for granted, forget what really matters, and forge ahead without acknowledging our accomplishments or basking in the blessings of our lives.

It takes only a moment for our reality to alter completely. In a moment, we can get fired from our jobs, infuse our children with insecurities, put ourselves in debt, or fall prey to a temptation that will destroy our lives. In a second we can fall down and crack our head open, lose a loved one in an accident, find out our best friend has cancer, or discover that our partner has embezzled all the company's money. It takes only a second for our world to fall apart before our eyes, yet most of us will deny this fact and take what we have for granted. It's in our nature to believe that what we have in our lives will stay in them. Most of us have a great deal of denial about how fragile we are and how uncertain life can be.

Time is precious. And when we realize this, we become aware of the importance of claiming each moment. Every moment holds the potential for being memorable. We all have the power to stop what we are doing and look for a way to make each moment special. If we don't stop each day and claim some of these moments, they will pass us by, never to be found again. In making this the best year ever, we must seize every opportunity to relish the details of our lives. These special moments surround us and can range from the subtle—like watching the sunrise every morning in bed—to the extraordinary—like watching your child blow out the candles on her fourth birthday cake.

I came to understand the importance of claiming the moment when I met my fiancé, Gary. Gary stops all the time to claim the moment, to capture the sacredness of each experience, to take a snapshot—mental or otherwise—of where we are and what we are doing. He has an innate appreciation of the preciousness of each moment, and he goes out of his way to remember each one. One of his favorite expressions is "Life is not a motion picture but rather a series of Polaroids." No matter where we are or what is going on around us, Gary seeks out and captures these Polaroid moments.

Recently, I had the honor of leading a seven-day workshop aboard a cruise ship. Gary and I were together with many of the coaches whom I train and people who had come to participate in the seminar. We had an amazing and productive time, and as our trip was coming to an end, Gary asked me what I was going to remember about this cruise. He wanted to know which of the ten thousand moments we had shared were most special to me. I took a few minutes to think about his question and felt surprised when I realized that I could hardly remember any of what made this trip so special. The moments that had made it special were lost inside the blur of a week of dining, dancing, talking, sunning, and all the other great things we had done. But what Gary wanted to know was what specifically I would remember and be able to recall twelve months from now. Which of the experiences we had shared would be ingrained in my mind forever?

When I realized that I couldn't pinpoint exactly what had made this trip so special, I understood what Gary had been trying to teach me for over a year: If I didn't sharpen my focus and adjust the lens that I experienced my life through by claiming these moments as special and literally taking a mental snapshot of them, they would just get lost inside the memory called "That was great." It was startling to realize that although I had spent this entire week truly having the most fun I had had all year, there were few moments I had claimed deeply enough to remember them for the next five years.

As I sat on the deck looking out to sea, I realized just how many trips I had been on in my lifetime that I had no specific memories of. Yes, I could remember the donkey ride in Santorini from fifteen years ago, but I couldn't remember who was with me or where we went or what had made it so special. Of course, there are many episodes in my life that I remember precisely, but they were monumental events that I will never forget—like when my son was born or my first book was published. But what was finally sinking in, after much prodding and commitment on Gary's part, is that each day offers some moment that is special. It might be my son saying something cute to me, someone acknowledging how my work has helped them, or a friend and me sharing a coffee while looking out into one of La Jolla's beautiful days. It might be a simple conversation I have with my mother and the hug we give each other when we say good-bye. But unless I stop while the event is happening and actually claim the moment consciously, I will more than likely forget it. It will just get lost inside a sea of a thousand other memories and become a vague and insignificant part of my past.

So my work began. I was committed to remembering what about this cruise had been truly meaningful to me and making sure that I took the time to claim each moment and give each experience its rightful place in my long-term memory. To do this, I would have to distinguish the event, think about what had made it so special, and then take a snapshot inside my mind—who was there, what had happened, and what I wanted to remember about it. I sat thinking about the events of the past week and sifting through all the things we had done, looking for the special moments I wanted to claim as mine and keep for the rest of my life. I asked myself, "What experiences, what people, places, dinners, or night activities, have made this trip so special?" After ten minutes of going through all the activities day by day, I realized there were several events that I wanted and needed to claim if they were to live on inside of my very full mind. I wanted to vividly remember the night Gary and I sat out on the deck and watched Mars—which was closer to the earth than it had been in sixty thousand years—light up the sky, turning it a deep shade of red as the wind blew, the clouds came in, and the rain began to fall. I realized that if I didn't claim that night right now, and make a mental snapshot of the experience, that night would be lost forever. Of course, something could happen in the future that would trigger the memory, but this was a moment so special that I didn't want to leave anything to chance. This was just one of many memorable moments I claimed that day.

Your best year will be made up of a collection of these moments that you claim as special and imprint into your consciousness. When you claim the moment, a few things happen: First, you take notice of all the good that is happening in your life right now. Second, you recognize events and things that happen in your life on a regular basis that you may take for granted. And, third—possibly the most important—claiming the moment has you take responsibility for creating these special moments. It has you search out and find these special events and value them. Floating across the screen of my computer are the words *Claim This Moment*. Because if I have the aware-ness and the discipline to claim even two special moments each day, by the end of the week I will have fourteen—and, by the end of the year, seven hundred twenty-eight—significant moments inside my memory that I can use to declare this the best year of my life.

Moments are moments and events are events, but they become special when we recognize that not one of them will ever come again, when we are keenly aware of the pre-ciousness of the event and choose to identify and label it as special enough to be remembered. For example, when we're taking the same old walk with the same friends and look up to see a hawk hovering above us, we can stop for a minute and admire the beauty of nature; then we can look around at the people we're with, appreciate the role they play in our lives, take a deep breath, and claim the moment. With the intention of anchoring the memory into our consciousness, we might have the urge to give them a hug or express our appreciation for them.

When we are committed to claiming the moment, we look upon, create, and invent our ordinary experience as something extraordinary. We become a magnet for the unique and special. The lens through which we view life shifts, and we become seekers of the divine in every moment. To see with new eyes, to become aware of the blessings we hold, to create new intimate moments each day—these constitute a spiritual quest. This is the art of making the ordinary moments of your life extraordinary.

Do It! Claim the Moment

Begin bringing more conscious awareness to the moments of your day. When you find yourself living a moment that has special significance, stop and breathe it in. Say to yourself, either silently or out loud, "I'm going to claim this moment." Then allow yourself to linger in that experience a little longer than usual, to notice what is special about it. Soak the moment in and consciously register it rather than rushing off to the next moment.

Consider what it would take for you to look for, create, and claim memorable moments every single day. What would you have to look for? What part of your awareness would have to shift? Find at least two moments each day to claim as your own.

_____

TEN

Creating Unforgettable Days

As important as claiming the moment is for creating your best year, planning unforgettable days is essential in creating a memorable and fulfilling life. To understand the value of a memorable day, all you have to do is ask yourself, "What would I do if this were the last year of my life? Would I continue to live each day as I lived today? Would I be spending my time the way I am right now?" Take a moment, stop reading, and ponder the following question: If you could live this past week over again, would you choose to live each day exactly as it was, or would you choose to live any of them differently?

Most of us won't allow ourselves to look at our lives through this retrospective lens. Although we know it to be true, most of us can't fully comprehend that we have only so many days on this planet. Instead, thanks to our innate and protective denial of death, we prefer to pretend that we have all the time in the world to do whatever we want. We live in the illusion that someday we will go on that trip, take a walk on the beach, read that book, go to the park with our children, or learn how to tango. We put off what we could do today for some future time that may never come.

Of course, there are particular days in our lives when we remember every detail, from the moment we wake up to the moment we go to sleep. Maybe it was our wedding day, the day our child was born, the day we graduated, the day we fell in love, the first time we made love, or the day we accomplished a job we had worked long and hard at. But, put to the test, most of us can't remember what we did last week, last month, or last year. Our days are a blur, one rolling into the next. Most of us will forget today by the time tomorrow comes, unless it is infused with some special significance.

So today I am going to ask you to honestly assess your life over the past five years and see how many special days you remember. How many days pop into your awareness that could have just been ordinary days but that, because of some commitment or declaration on your part, you made special enough that you can recall them right here in this moment? Maybe you've already experienced the sweet satisfaction of drifting off to sleep many nights this year knowing that you lived a day you will never forget. But I am going to ask you to look and see how many days you would want to remember from this year. How many days do you want to label as extraordinary and have as sealed experiences that can be shared and passed down for generations?

Close your eyes for a moment and remember a story that one of your parents shared with you about a day in their lives that was significant. What was so special about this day? The stories that get passed down and shared are often about ordinary days when someone did something great for someone else, or when our families were all together, enjoying each other's company. When a special gift was shared or words were exchanged that touched another's heart. Food fights, camping trips, and over-night parties are often recalled when reminiscing about the past.

So what determines the making of an unforgettable day? To log a great day into your consciousness, first and foremost it must touch your heart. It must evoke strong positive emotions such as joy, happiness, or deep appreciation. Negative events that cause us emotional distress are often easier to remember, because these events often have some shock to them that glues them into our memory. To create that same charge for our positive events, we must venture outside what we know and what is comfortable for us to feel. This often entails doing something that will leave us feeling a little vulnerable, something that is outside our comfort zone. To create unforgettable days, we have to rise above the mundane and design these special days with significant gestures. If you take a moment to think back to some of the memorable days in your life, you will probably discover that they involved some degree of risk or vulnerability. Careful planning and thoughtfulness are also characteristic of unforget-table days. By overcoming the pull of the safe and the ordinary, we can create a day that will leave an indelible impression in our consciousness.

During one of the "Best Year of Your Life" training sessions that I lead, Dez decided she wanted the three people in her life that are most important to her to feel her love and deep appreciation for them. She had little time and a small budget, so she decided she would make dinner for her husband and daughters and then write something to each of them to share her love. She then went out and bought some flowers, deciding that she would sprinkle rose petals on the table before serving dinner and sharing her words. Feeling very vulnerable and uncomfortable, Dez took the time to create a special atmosphere by putting on some soft music and lighting a few candles, so they would all know that something out of the ordinary was about to take place. Then, one by one, she sat in front of the three people she loves the most in the world and delivered her heart to them in words, actions, tears, and hugs. When she was done, she knew that she would remember that evening for the rest of her life—and to this day, she still does.

So often we have great ideas of how to lavish love upon those we care for, but we feel uncomfortable going over the top. Yet to ensure that we have a day that will last a lifetime, we must do something that is outside the box to make it memorable.

Creating an unforgettable day does not have to take a lot of time or money. You can declare Saturday "laugh day" and take your kids to the video store and rent a few funny movies. Then you could cuddle up on the couch, make some popcorn, turn down the lights, and spend the day as a family, doing nothing but laughing. If you had a laugh day with your parents when you were a child, wouldn't you remember it? You could do what one of my friends did and take out an ad in the shape of a heart in your local paper, expressing your undying love for your husband or wife. Then pack up a picnic lunch, a card, and a book of poems and declare it a "romance day." I don't know anyone who wouldn't want to be the recipient of that! Or you could bring some flowers, a bottle of wine, and your favorite board game to the home of a friend you don't spend enough time with and create an unforgettable day with them. You might plan a "family day" and have everyone in your family bring photos that aren't in albums, make everyone's favorite desserts, and sit around and tell stories by looking at the pictures and creating photo albums to last a lifetime.

We can always find an excuse for why today couldn't possibly be an unforgettable day. Look at the reasons and excuses you come up with that stop you from making this day extraordinary. Do you find yourself saying, "I'll do it tomorrow" or "I'll take a vacation with my kids next year"; "I'll spend alone time with my husband when the children are out of the house"; or, my favorite, "I'll do it when I have more time"?

What if creating an "off the charts" day was a practice you did for yourself every month? Some of us are good at doing things for others but cut corners when it comes to making our days alone special. If you're one of those people, creating an unforgettable day may require you to put down your to-do list and think of ways to lavish love upon yourself. Notice if you want to sell out on yourself and give yourself only a few hours or if you want to put it off. Notice if you minimize the importance of creating unforgettable days for yourself.

Choosing to create these unforgettable days for ourselves and others is an awesome task and a "must" if we are truly committed to creating the best year of our lives. Part of the joy of unforgettable days is sharing them with the people we love. Days that leave a lasting impression on us and others don't just come about simply because the sun is shining and everything in the outer world seems to be going our way. They are not the result of good luck or fate. Creating an abundance of best days this year will not just happen; they must be intended, planned, created, lived, and then declared.

If taking the risk to make a day special could touch someone to the point of sheer ecstasy, and inspire them to go out and affect another—well, wouldn't that be incredibly exciting and fulfilling? Isn't that worth the effort? The whole idea of "paying it forward" and creating a domino effect of love and joy is the mission of creating the best year of our lives. Most of us are waiting for the right time or the right moment to make our days special. What would happen if you stopped waiting, if you seized the day and took responsibility for shifting your experience right now? Would an abundance of unforgettable days lead you to the best year of your life?

Do It! Create Unforgettable Days

Plan one day every month to be a day you will never forget. Consider what would make this day so special that you would clearly remember it for the rest of your life. Give yourself permission to lavish love upon yourself and those you care about. Enroll your family and friends to participate in these days with you. Practice turning ordinary times into fun, unforgettable days.

ELEVEN

Living Your Life as an Example

I remember a time when I wanted desperately to make some major changes in my life. I had been searching for years, trying to figure out how I could be happier, more fulfilled, and peaceful. I wanted to be great, to find more meaning in my life, and to express my best self, but something would always sidetrack me from fulfilling my deepest desires and I would end up repeating the same patterns year after year. Whenever I began to take steps in the right direction, something would happen that would divert me from continuing on the road to success and I would suddenly do something to sabotage myself. Instead of thriving, I became just another person surviving life. My friends, family, and co-workers could not figure out why I was always creating huge distractions that turned me away from the road to my dreams.

Then, one day, it finally occurred to me that I didn't think I deserved more happiness and success than I already had. It became glaringly obvious that my self-sabotaging behaviors were a way to punish myself for my perceived flaws and past mistakes. No matter how hard I tried, I couldn't seem to commit to having it all and being the best person I could possibly be. I couldn't muster up the motivation, even though I wanted with all my heart to make lasting changes. Then, one day, as I was taking some time to sit quietly, I heard a voice inside me say, "Don't become the greatest person you can be for yourself. Do it for someone else. Do it for the people who look up to you and admire you. Do it for the kids who think they aren't good enough. Do it so other people will see that they, too, can be great." Suddenly I understood a truth I had heard so many times before: Each of our lives matter and make a huge difference in this world, and each of us has the opportunity to make this world a better place. I felt inspired, and the procrastination and resignation that seemed to always follow me around were now replaced by an excitement and enthusiasm for my own life. I felt that a long-buried truth had been revealed to me and I now understood how I could make a bigger contribution to the world. All I had to do was be the best "me" I could possibly be and show others by example that they can do it, too. If I couldn't do it for myself, then fine; I could make my mark in the world by doing it for someone else.

If becoming your most extraordinary self doesn't inspire you, if claiming your greatness doesn't get you moving in the morning, if you don't think you are worthy of going after your best life, then dedicate this year to someone else and make it your best for them. Do it for your children, a niece, a nephew, or someone in need of a positive role model. Look around you and see who in your life will benefit by your taking yourself to the next level of greatness. You can pick someone you love or someone you don't even know; it doesn't matter as long as they would benefit from your example and support. Go to www.mentoring.org and volunteer as a mentor; do it for that child. Choose a specific person, group, or organization and dedicate the best year of your life to them.

Just imagine what would be possible if every person who interacts with you this year could see and feel your greatness. What if they could see the light in your eyes, hear the gratitude in your voice, and experience your total and complete enthusiasm for life? Do you think that would make a difference for them? What if this was your only purpose, your task to complete this year? What if all you needed to do was to live your life in such a way that you inspired others to become enthusiastic about their own lives and share their gifts with those around them? If you are willing to reach your full potential, if you're willing to go after your dreams and create them, what are you teaching those around you? You are teaching them, of course, that they, too, have the power to make their dreams come true. That they, too, are worthy of living their best life. You never know; the person you choose to mentor could go out and change the world. They may find the courage to do something extraordinary with their life because you modeled that courage to them. As a teacher, I am awed every day by the people around me who are taking on tasks and changing the world because they realized that if I could do it, they could do it as well. This is the power of living your life as an example.

I recently asked a group of my coaches who were doing an advanced training with me to live the best year of their lives in order to provide an example of what is possible for someone they love. Kathy, by nature shy and withdrawn, committed to living her best life and standing up for what she believes, for the sake of her son, Andrew, who shared her tendency to be soft-spoken and introverted.

One day, Kathy, her son, and her friend Alice were all having lunch together when Alice made a remark that Kathy felt was inappropriate. Although in the past she would have kept quiet and quickly dismissed the comment, Kathy remembered her commitment to bringing forth her best self for the sake of her son and decided to speak out. She told her friend that she thought her comment was inappropriate and asked her in the future to keep her opinions to herself. Kathy felt proud of herself for having set a strong boundary, but didn't give a second thought to the impact it might have on her son.

The very next week, Andrew came home from school and excitedly told his mom how he had stood up in class and voiced his opinion about something that mattered to him. Stunned, Kathy asked him, "What made you decide to stand up and speak out?" Andrew replied, "I did it because I saw you stand up to Alice." From that day on, Kathy carefully considered her choices and actions, knowing that how she lived her life impacted the way Andrew chose to live his. Kathy was no longer willing to overlook things or withhold her point of view, because she was committed to being an example to her son.

Dedicating your life and your daily choices to something greater than yourself allows you to keep getting out of your own way and demands the best of who you are to come forth. Using your success to benefit another is the greatest gift you can give—not only to them but to yourself.

By the time he was in his mid-forties, Ray was a prominent and influential businessman who had already attained a level of success he had never dreamed possible. Shortly after making one of the biggest business deals of his career, Ray realized that no matter how many deals he closed or how much money he made, success alone left him feeling unfulfilled. It was thus at the height of his career that Ray made an important discovery that changed his life and ultimately the lives of countless others: The more he reached out and contributed to the lives of others, the more happiness and fulfillment he felt. Ray got involved in the Boys and Girls Club and created a program where children who normally wouldn't be able to afford college would have their tuition paid if they maintained good grades in high school. He continued to follow his passion for helping others, and what began as a commitment to mentor just a few children evolved into the development of the National Mentoring Partnership, which today is the leading national movement connecting America's young people with caring adult mentors. This man who already possessed everything money could buy now possesses one of life's greatest secrets: that being of service is a gift that you give not only to others, but also to yourself.

On the days when you feel like you can't do it or you don't want to try again or you are about to enter into something that threatens to sabotage your success, you can remember that you're committed to living your best life for the sake of someone other than just yourself. This will give you the strength and the inspiration to make a higher choice.

Imagine what this world would be like if each of us lived our lives in the service of others. If we each understood that those we love learn by watching us, we would probably become far more conscious of all that we do. If we were each aware of how much our success contributes to others, we might not get so caught up in "I'm too scared" or "I'm too busy" or "I'm too tired." What if making your life extraordinary would save a child's life? If you knew that to be the case, wouldn't you figure out how to do it? Of course you would. You would do whatever you had to do to make peace with your past, to make empowering choices, to be compassionate to yourself and those around you. You would do it because you had to. How about if this year you pretend that you have to?

I know for myself that the times when I'm most joyful are when I'm teaching or involved in a project bigger than myself. When I am actively making this world a better place, purpose and contentment permeate every cell in my body. This is true for most of us. Last year I led a weeklong intensive workshop for a group of fifty people who were training to become coaches using the techniques and processes I teach. On the third day we went around the group, and each of the trainees shared what they were committed to creating in their lives as a result of their training. One by one, they spoke of results like losing weight, getting a certain number of new clients, having more love, and on and on. By about the twenty-fifth coach, I couldn't go on any further. I felt tired, as if my energy was leaving my body. There was no vitality, no passion, and absolutely no joy in what they were sharing, and I knew that without that level of enthusiasm there was no way any of these amazing individuals could deliver the extraordinary gifts they were meant to give to the world. I sat down, saddened by the fact that after all of the work I had done with them over the past several years, these coaches were still myopically focused on all-about-me goals.

Because I am driven to support people in transforming themselves, I knew I had to do something drastic. I stopped what we were doing and split the group into smaller groups, instructing them that on their lunch break each group was to create a project that would contribute to someone or something other than themselves—whether it was a home for the elderly, a shelter for homeless families, or a children's charity. The only criteria were that it had to inspire everyone in the group, it had to be a call to service, and it had to be achievable within one month.

After lunch the group returned smiling and chatting, and you could actually feel the surge of electricity, excitement, and boundless energy filling up the room. Group by group they stood up and shared what we termed their "holiday projects" (since they were to be completed by December 31). Jennifer, Debbie, Shadi, Loree, and Shendl founded the Seagull Project, whose stated mission was "to assist women in connecting with their confidence, pride, and dignity by supporting them in transitioning back into the workplace." The pride and joy they exuded after sharing their mission statement was heightened when one month later, on a follow-up call, they shared with me how easily they had accomplished this great task and how it brought them closer to all of the people in their lives as they invited them to join in and help.

Rachel and Rochelle, who called themselves the Gifts of Love, committed to creating a lavish holiday party, complete with entertainment, food, and presents, for those without a home. Their mission was to provide people in crisis with an experience of joy, celebration, and the feeling of being loved as they would at a family holiday. This group met with the directors of Safe Space, a shelter for women and children who have escaped domestic violence, and made arrangements for the holiday party. They sent all the women invitations, decorated the room, and brought in two manicurists, a professional makeup artist, a massage therapist (some of these women had never had a loving-touch massage), a karaoke singer, and Italian food from a popular local restaurant. They arranged for someone to dress up in a donated Santa costume and hand out gifts to the children. A local high-fashion boutique gladly donated hundreds of dollars' worth of clothes, and a professional stylist spent hours setting up a temporary boutique to give each of the women gifts of clothes, jewelry, perfume, and makeup—all donated by people excited to share what they had. The night of the party, this group sang, said prayers, played games, and danced the night away. One of the women guests, with tears in her eyes, said that it was the first time she had felt happiness in a very long time. Everyone involved in this project had donated their time and energy, yet they left the event more fulfilled than when they had arrived. The delight of the children and the laughter and tears of the women left them filled with gratitude and love in their hearts, knowing they had made a very great difference in the lives of these beautiful but hurting souls.

These are just two examples of what got birthed out of a group of committed individuals from all over the world. All it took was an intention to serve others and a commitment to making a contribution. In all my years as a teacher, the one thing I have learned is that people love to make a difference in the world. They love to know that they matter. They love to feel useful and important. They love being part of making this world a better place. People want to contribute, because it brings them great joy. As the great poet Rabindranath Tagore wrote, "I slept and dreamt that life was joy. I awoke and saw that life was service. I acted and behold, service was joy."

This is how each of us can make the world a better place. We can commit to letting go of our emotional baggage in the name of someone else. We can let go of the everyday burdens that squash our joy and replace them with an unwavering commitment to others who are less fortunate than ourselves. We can become a mentor or volunteer for an organization in need of support. When we make a commitment to living in service of the greater whole, we also commit to living a life filled with joy and gratitude. The gifts we will receive for dedicating our lives to another are priceless.

Do It!
Live Your Life as an Example

Consider the people whose lives will be most impacted if you successfully create this as the best year of your life. Choose a person, group, or organization to dedicate the next year to and commit yourself to being an inspiring example of what's possible for that person or group. Keep a picture of the person or group of people where you will see it often and ask yourself on a daily basis what you can do each day to make your life extraordinary, knowing that you are teaching others that they too can do so.

TWELVE

Aspiring to Excellence

We live in a world where it's so easy to be ordinary. Mediocrity is the language of the land, and it seems that most of us are resigned to living well below our potential. But it's important to realize that this wasn't always the case. There was a time in most of our lives when we aspired to excellence. We had a natural competitiveness and confidence. We knew that we could do or create whatever we set our minds to, and we were willing to stand out from the crowd. We had the courage to sing at the top of our lungs, to demonstrate our skills. Quite simply, we believed in ourselves.

If we're going to make this the best year of our lives, we must reclaim our innate desire for excellence. We must muster up the courage to go out and make the most of every day. We must look at life through new eyes—eyes that see possibility where there was none before, eyes that see greatness and stay focused on long-term fulfillment rather than short-term gratification. To create a life beyond what we know, we must have the courage to listen to others intently, to hear their needs and their concerns. We must take the time to listen to the cries of our own soul and have the faith to make changes and take risks. We must open our hearts where they've previously been closed and find forgiveness and compassion for those in need of our love. Excellence requires us to have the courage to give up how we have lived our lives up to this point and go after something that is totally unknown.

To live a life of excellence, you will have to take risks. You will have to step into new territory and climb new mountains. If you're up to something that's as big as you are, it's going to be scary. If it feels perfectly safe, you are probably underachieving. To leave your mark in the world, you will have to stand someplace you've never been willing to stand before. And you will have to have the courage to aspire to excellence. To create an extraordinary life you will have to be present in each moment and give 100 percent of yourself. You will have to commit each day to being the best you can be, and aspire to perform your daily tasks in the most conscious way possible. Living your best year requires you to take a moment each time you're about to make a move—whether you are about to deliver a communication, make a decision, or put something into your body—and make sure that move reflects the very highest choice you could make. It's a year to aspire to excellence in all areas of your life, to slow down if you're moving too fast and make sure that each move you make is taking you in the direction of your dreams. Aspiring to excellence is a commitment that you must make each day when you open your eyes. This commitment will lift you out of ordinary action and empower you to take extraordinary action. It will call on you to show up for your life as you never have before in order to make your dreams a reality.

You might be thinking that it's too hard and will take too much effort to give 100 percent, but I promise you that if you are underachieving, playing small, withholding your gifts, or making choices that disempower you, you are probably already exhausted. Denying your greatness and quashing your natural potential is hard work. It actually takes more energy to live a less than satisfying life than it does to live a fantastically exciting one. How can that be? you might ask. Well, let's talk about it. When you're passionate about what you're doing, when you're engaging your whole body, mind, and soul in the task at hand, you fill yourself up with a high positive energy that replenishes you rather than depletes you. Every time you make the choice to bring forth your best, you release good feelings inside of yourself that fill you up and lift your spirits. And when your spirits are lifted, you naturally have more energy. Think about a time when you fell in love. Were you tired and drowsy? Only if you stayed up all night with your lover having fun or talking endlessly. Otherwise, you could dance until the sun came up, sing in the shower, and smile at everyone you saw no matter what they were doing. It takes no effort to sustain this energy, because it is a naturally effortless state.

When you're excited and energized about your life, the world and everyone in it is gorgeous. You see solutions and possibilities. You are in the flow; you're enthused, passionate, and in love. You're at peace with yourself. When you make choices that reflect your intent to have the best year of your life, your internal process shifts completely and you have access to resources that were previously unavailable. When you're playing full-out, you naturally feel inspired about your life. On the other hand, when you're playing small you feel tired and bored. When you're looking at your life through a limited perspective, you can't see all the possibilities that exist for you. Remember the old expression "You have to put your best foot forward." The reason this expression has been around for so long is that it's true! If you put your best foot forward, you will be rewarded. If you do your part, if you take one step toward expressing all the greatness that lives within you, the universe will take a hundred steps toward you. But *you* must be willing to take the first step.

I lead my "Shadow Process" workshop several times a year, and on the second night we do a very powerful anger-release exercise. We take all the chairs out of the room. Then each participant finds a place to stand and puts on a blindfold so they are focused entirely on themselves. The lights in the room are dimmed, and the music in the background is turned up. We begin by doing some deep breathing, and then we change the music to something a little more intense and everyone is given the opportunity to scream, yell, or just shake their fists. It's intended to release the repressed energy that blocks us from having access to all of our power, self-expression, and greatness. We typically have well over a hundred people in the room during this exercise, and I am always amazed to see the different ways in which people respond to the process. Even after an hour's preparation and my encouraging them to give their all and, if they need to, to fake it till they make it, some people just stand there, as if frozen, and do nothing at all. Some people make a modest attempt toward finding their energy and their passion. Others appear to be waiting for someone to do it for them, resisting any support or help from the staff. And then there are those courageous, focused individuals who come in committed to doing whatever it takes to break through the limitations that have held them back and come face-to-face with the power of their true self. The results always speak for themselves. The people who come in and go full-out say it's one of the most powerful experiences of their entire lives, while those who barely make an effort don't really get it. I've never seen one person who comes in giving 100 percent who doesn't get exactly what they came for.

I share with you this example to reinforce the fact that the universe can give us only what we give ourselves. If we are unwilling to make the effort, to show up completely, to give our all, it is impossible for the world around us to give us what we want. Even if others try for our benefit, even if the universe conspires to give us what we cannot give ourselves, we will fail to recognize it—even when it lands on our doorstep.

It's our responsibility to bring forth our greatness. At birth we are given the awesome privilege of enjoying this world. For most of us, the joy left when we were young and the fight to survive began. Now is the time to recognize that there are only so many breaths each of us will breathe. There are only so many moments each of us will get to experience. There are only so many days, months, and years each of us will live. So why not choose today to make each moment great? Why not begin to choose excellence in everything you do? What would be available to you now and in the future if you began waking up each morning with a commitment to excellence and living your greatest life?

When we are living each day to its fullest, our appreciation for life explodes. And by living each day to its fullest I don't mean getting everything on your to-do list done. I mean finding joy in the moment and having passion for the tasks at hand. When we aspire to excellence, we bring forth all of our attention when we are speaking to our children, friends, and loved ones. We naturally slow down to breathe in the fresh air when we step outside. We recognize that this is our only opportunity to live today and express ourselves completely. This is our opportunity to be great. There is no dress rehearsal here on earth, so we can either go out and give our best performance—winning ourselves a gold medal, so to speak—in this lifetime, or we can idly sit by, wishing, wanting, and wondering, Why me? At the end of the day our life is in our hands. What will you do with yours?

Do It! Aspire to Excellence

Recall a time when you were passionate about a cause, put forth your best effort, and aspired to excellence. What commitment will you need to make today in order to bring forth this degree of excellence in every area of your life?

RESOURCES

None of us achieve great success by ourselves. These are the people along my path who have supported me in creating a life beyond my wildest dreams. I offer you this list and encourage you to use these resources to support you in living a life beyond what you believe is possible for yourself. My heartfelt appreciation goes to each and every person along my path—both on and off this list—who helped me to become the person I am today.

John F. Kennedy University, one of the most innovative universities in the world: www.jfku.edu.

John F. Kennedy University, a leader in holistic studies and leading-edge education, is now offering many of my programs as part of their accredited Coach Training program. Details of our joint programs can be found at www.jfku.edu/ford.

Deepak Chopra, M.D., David Simon, M.D., and The Chopra Center for Well Being, who offer a collection of teachings that translate ancient Vedic wisdom into practical life-changing tools: www.chopra.com.

The Center for Authentic Leadership, founded by Jan Smith, my greatest teacher and a leading-edge thinker: www.authentic-leadership.com.

The Hoffman Quadrinity Process, which teaches a life-changing psychological process to heal the wounds of your past: www.quadrinity.com.

Landmark Education, which delivers innovative, life-transforming courses to support you in living more powerfully in the world: www.landmarkeducation.com.

The Psychosynthesis Process, a process that changed my life: www.psychosynthesis.edu.

The writings and teachings of Jeremiah Abrams, my friend, mentor, and therapist extraordinaire: www.mtvision.org.

The work of Marianne Williamson, whose books offer new spiritual perspectives and inspirational wisdom: www.marianne.com.

The work of Cheryl Richardson, whose practical everyday approach to life will set you on the road to success: www.cheryl-richardson.com.

The Spiritual Cinema Circle, which delivers movies to your home every month that will entertain, enlighten, and inspire you: www.spiritualcinemacircle.com/bestyear.

Alanis Morissette, whose latest album, *So Called Chaos,* is designed to expand your consciousness and heal your heart: www.alanis.com.

The Sedona Method, by Hale Dwoskin, a process that can help you release negative emotions and create the life you desire: www.sedonamethod.com.

The Relationship Solution, created by Gay and Katie Hendricks, a comprehensive course for enhancing love in your life: www.therelationshipsolution.com.

Susanne West, a wise and creative coach who is great at facilitating seminars and also offers individual coaching: www.susannewest.com.

Amma, one of the few living saints, offers spiritual retreats around the world. Visit www.amma.org.

The Shadow Process Workshop, a three-day heart-opening experience that I personally guarantee will change your life: www.shadowprocess.com.

Integrative Coaching, a process that can transform your life and unleash your greatest potential. Visit www.integrative-coaching.com to train to become—or to hire—one of the best coaches in the field.

Life Beyond Beliefs, an eight-week tele-class that supports you in stepping out of your self-imposed limitations while guiding you to access all of your untapped potential: www.integrativecoaching.com.

Essentials for an Extraordinary Life, a ten-week tele-class offered over the phone, that supports you in creating the best year of your life: www.bestyearofyourlife.com.

Essentials Coaching, which equips you with the "essential" skills and techniques to create an extraordinary life. Visit www.bestyearofyourlife.com to find the perfect coach for you.

ACKNOWLEDGMENTS

I am blessed to have at my side some of the most dedicated, soulful, and talented people. Each of them, in their own way, supports me in creating every year to be better than the last.

To Arielle Ford and Brian Hilliard, my agents and managers, for standing by my work in the world and lovingly urging me to do more.

To my loving, supportive, and tireless staff, whose contributions are countless. To Danielle Dorman, my awesomely talented friend and editor who I could not live without. You are truly one in a million and I feel so blessed to have you at my side. To Cliff Edwards and Rachel Levy for your special contributions to this book. To Donna Lipman and Jeff Malone for your brilliance, creativity, and devotion. To the entire staff of the Institute for Integrative Coaching—Angela Delayni-Hart, Anne Browning, Candy Spahr, Pam Nelson, and Donna Baker—for living this work day in and day out while coaching others to do the same. To Adam

Heller, Diann Craven, Sharon Keefer, Debra Evans, Dave and Debbie Charlton, and Loree Oberle-Edwards, who have given so much of your time and hearts to this work. To Geeta Singh of the Talent Exchange for all your care and diligence.

My heartfelt thanks goes out to Julia Aspinwall, Lizbeth Garcia, and all those who have participated in my programs for sharing your stories, trials and tribulations, and amazing successes. And to the hundreds of Certified Integrative and Essentials coaches who support people all over the world in fulfilling their deepest desires, thank you for living your lives as an example of what is possible.

To my very special friend, Alanis Morissette, for singing your soul's message so loud and supporting me in so many ways in getting my messages out into the world.

To Randy Thomas, who not only delivered me the man of my dreams, but continually holds me in the highest vision of my life.

To my loving and supportive family, who stand by me each and every day. To my remarkable son, Beau, who makes my life a joyous wonderland; my mother, whose undying love and organizational skills keep me sane; and to my incredible nieces and nephews for being living examples of excellence. To my new family, who have already brought me a whole new level of joy and contentment: my incredibly talented stepsons,

Brandon and Stephen Ravet; my loving and caring new in-laws, Shirl and Manny Ravet; and the rest of the family, Deborah, Laurel, Lorey, John, Jillian, Patty, Bruce, and Bryan. Wow, you are one sensational, inspiring family!

To Bryan Vess, Dan Schroebel, and Pamela Forelich, a team of outstanding professionals who have contributed so much to the quality of my life this year. Thank you for making me the lucky beneficiary of your high standards and impeccability.

To Alisha Schwartz, Allison Bechill, and Caline Assilian, the caring young women who have taken such great care of Beau and me this year. Your support provides the solid foundation that enables me to do what I do in the world. Thank you. To Jeremiah Sullivan for always making me smile for the camera.

And most of all to Gideon Weil, my fantastic new editor whose contributions were tremendous, and to Margery Buchanan, Claudia Riemer Boutote, Miki Terasawa, Carl Walesa, Lisa Zuniga, and the rest of the amazing staff at HarperSanFrancisco.

ABOUT THE AUTHOR

Debbie Ford is a #1 *New York Times* bestselling author whose books are translated into twenty-six languages and used as teaching tools in universities and other institutions of learning and enlightenment worldwide. Her first three books, *The Dark Side of the Light Chasers, Spiritual Divorce,* and *The Secret of the Shadow,* teach readers how to access their inner wisdom and receive insights about their lives by going within. Her fourth book, *The Right Questions,* shows readers how to turn their insights into action by giving them the practical tools to make life-changing choices.

In this book, *The Best Year of Your Life,* Debbie unveils the proven formula for creating an extraordinary life, guiding you to step into your greatness and develop the aspects of yourself that will ensure your success. Her desire is to create a worldwide movement, enrolling millions of people to make this the best year of their lives. Please visit www.bestyearofyourlife.com for details.

Debbie earned a degree in psychology with an emphasis in consciousness studies from JFK University, and in 2001 received the Alumni of the Year Award for her outstanding contribution in the fields of psychology and spirituality. She was awarded an honorary Doctorate from Emerson University in 2003, and in 2004 she received an honorary Doctorate of Humane Letters from the John F. Kennedy University Board of Regents.

As the founder of the Ford Institute for Integrative Coaching (www.integrativecoaching.com), Debbie has developed ground-breaking coaching techniques that have been studied and used by individuals across the world. She is the creator and leader of the Shadow Process (www.shadowprocess.com), a three-day life-altering workshop that has transformed the lives of tens of thousands of people worldwide.

Debbie has been featured numerous times on *Oprah* and *Good Morning America*, and is a welcomed return guest on radio and morning shows across the country. Her insightful teachings and revolutionary inner processes, combined with her intolerance for mediocrity, have made her an internationally renowned coach, motivational speaker, and seminar leader.

To arrange for Debbie to speak at your conference or event, go to www.debbieford.com. To receive her action-oriented weekly Best Year of Your Life e-newsletter, please register at www.bestyearofyourlife.com.